OPPOSING FORCES

Alexei Navalny
Adam Michnik

Foreword by Daniel Treisman

Egret Press

Copyright © 2015 Alexei Navalny, Adam Michnik
The right of Alexei Navalny, Adam Michnik, and Daniel Treisman
to be identified as the Authors of the Work has been asserted by
them in accordance with the Copyright, Designs and Patents Act
1988.

First published in Russian by Novoe Izdatelstvo
(New Press), Moscow 2015

First published in translation in Great Britain
in 2016 by EGRET PRESS

Cataloguing in Publication data is available
from the British Library

ISBN 978-0-9933869-3-0

Translated by Leo Shtutin
Editors: Jeremy Noble, Vladimir Ashurkov, Laura Gozzi

Cover design by Stuart Bache
Typeset in 10½ pt Times New Roman
by Geoff Fisher geoff.fisher@yahoo.co.uk

Printed and bound in Great Britain by
CPI Group (UK), Croydon CR4 4YY

All rights reserved. Apart from any use permitted by UK copyright
law, no parts of this book may be reproduced in any form or by any
means without written consent from the publishers or, in the case of
reprographic production, in accordance with the terms of licences
issued by the Copyright Licensing Agency

Egret's policy is to use papers that are natural, renewable and
recyclable products, made from wood grown in sustainable forests.
The logging and manufacturing processes are expected to conform
to the environmental regulations of the country of origin.

EGRET PRESS
London

Contents

Editor's Note	v
Foreword by Daniel Treisman	vii
Introduction by Alexei Navalny	xxi
Introduction by Adam Michnik	xxiii
1. From Dissidents to Solidarity	1
2. Battling the Regime	9
3. Solidarity comes to Power	19
4. Lustration	28
5. Gorbachev, Yeltsin, and Putin	35
6. Corruption as an Institution	50
7. The Russian Idea	56
8. Nationalism	62
9. The Church and Fundamentalism	73
10. The Path to Europe	86
11. Russia and Ukraine	98
12. Rewriting History	111
About the Interlocutors	
Alexei Navalny	119
Adam Michnik	119
Daniel Treisman (Foreword)	120
Glossary	121
Endnotes	147

Editor's Note
Jeremy Noble

The written record of an animated discussion in Red Square, between a Russian and a Pole, talking about any number of controversial matters, within sight (and probably hearing) of the Kremlin, was always going to cause consternation and not a little excitement. But the editor's task is to elucidate and adjudicate, not to exclaim and judge – that can be left to the reader.

Grateful thanks should go first to Daniel Treisman for agreeing to write the foreword, which elegantly places the discussion between Alexei Navalny and Adam Michnik both in its historical and contemporary context.

In the course of these perambulations around Red Square, many people, historical and living, are mentioned, some in passing, some in depth. It was felt that one could not decide how many of these people would be known to the reader; and at the risk of somebody exclaiming "I know who Gorbachev is!" there is an extensive glossary of (hopefully all) the people discussed, and sometimes dissed. Likewise, there are a, by no means exhaustive, number of endnotes, the purpose of which is to give to the reader just as much background as might be necessary to shed light on an event, no matter if it took place recently or in the dim and distant past.

Which brings one to the biggest editorial conumdrum of all – spelling. Does one write Lvov? Lviv? *Lwów*? Since we're talking about the Polish perspective …; and what about Vilnius vs *Wilno?* Oh, the arguments there have been about a particular spelling; this one signifying support of Russian imperialism, that one trampling on the sensitivities of the Poles, another one ignoring the yearnings of the

Ukrainians ... The result was that the only consensus to be found lay in choosing whatever spelling the reader would likely find most familiar (then why not, one asks, "Alexander" instead of "Aleksandr ...").

If only an editor could be as brave as Alexei Navalny and Adam Michnik, when it comes to words, but an editor has no place behind the barricades, rather, one takes shelter behind the full stop.

Foreword
Daniel Treisman

There are moments in unfree societies when the perceptions of millions suddenly converge. A controversial article slips through the censor's net and sparks conversations nationwide. A tiny protest metamorphoses into a multi-city uprising. Always unexpected, such events tend to develop rapidly, like a crisis on the stock exchange.

Whatever the details, such moments are, first and foremost, moments of mutual recognition. Citizens realise they are not alone; they constitute a group, a class, a nation. A community – sometimes for the first time – *sees* itself. And that experience of seeing and being seen is, in fact, what makes it a community.

The result is not necessarily a revolution or other political change. But such moments transform the social landscape, creating new actors and new consciousness. They show how the tectonic plates have shifted. Those in power often respond with violence. However, while clubs and threats can force people back into their apartments, it is much more difficult to erase their memory of the experience. One cannot shoot a moment. Once seen, a community is hard to unsee.

Something like this occurred in Moscow in December 2011. That winter, residents of the capital began to congregate in the city's central spaces. They came in tens – sometimes hundreds – of thousands. Previously apolitical lawyers, artists, lecturers, writers, businessmen, and many other members of a small but growing middle class found themselves thronging to such gathering points as Marsh Square – actually an avenue on a crescent-shaped river island – or the appropriately named Sakharov Prospect.

The trigger was the blatant fraud that hundreds of

volunteer observers had recorded during the recent parliamentary election. Protesters demanded a new ballot. But concerns soon broadened. Some began to call for President Putin's ousting. In the Kremlin, officials watched with confusion and then alarm.

Those who met in the squares came away changed. They saw others like themselves, thousands of them. The journalist Maxim Trudolyubov, strolling among the crowds, experienced a strange kind of déjà vu. He kept seeing faces that looked familiar although, he realised, most of them were not.

Many speakers addressed the meetings that winter – popular writers, leftists, nationalists, environmentalists even Putin's former finance minister, Alexei Kudrin. But the one who best caught the mood of the listeners was a 35-year-old activist named Alexei Navalny.

Forty-three years earlier, a similar moment of awakening had transfixed Warsaw. In January 1968, students mobbed the final performance of a production of *Dzyady*[1] [*Forefathers' Eve*], an epic drama by the 19th Century romantic bard Adam Mickiewicz. The Communist authorities had forced the theatre to cut short its run after audiences started cheering the play's anti-Russian allusions.

A 22-year-old history student named Adam Michnik reported the events to a journalist from *Le Monde*, whose account was then broadcast by Radio Free Europe. Michnik was expelled from the university and arrested. That March, Warsaw University students held a large demonstration in Michnik's defence, and to demand an end to censorship and

---

[1] Written in 1832, *Dzyady* [*Forefathers' Eve*] carried clear anti-imperial overtones, with Russophobic sentiments potentially discernible in it as well. Mickiewicz himself, however, denied such claims; around the same period, moreover, he composed "To my Russian Friends" – a poem eulogising the Decembrists.

Soviet domination. They were brutally suppressed by the riot police and "worker squads." Unexpectedly, student strikes broke out across the country, in Krakow, Poznan, and other university cities.

Last April, these two men met in Moscow for a series of informal discussions that stretched across three days. This book is the result. The genre is that of the recorded conversation, a literary form as characteristic of Eastern Europe as the absurdist novel or the anthology of "Letters from Prison." Listening in, one almost smells the espresso and cigarette smoke. Michnik is a master of the form. His past partners range from his friend Vaclav Havel to Poland's General Wojciech Jaruzelski, from fellow *soixante-huitards* Daniel Cohn-Bendit and Bernard Kouchner to the poet Czeslaw Milosz.

The meeting occurred at a gloomy time for the democratic opposition in Russia. The protests of December 2011 had petered out over the following year. A barrage of propaganda from the official media had incited fear and anger towards the West and rallied the public behind President Putin. To the delight of almost the entire population, Russia had torn Crimea from Ukraine and annexed it. And then, not long before Michnik and Navalny's conversations, their mutual friend, the Yeltsin-era politician and opposition leader Boris Nemtsov, had been brutally murdered, gunned down on a bridge beside the Kremlin.

Michnik's biography and writings are already familiar to many Western readers. Born into the stagnant Stalinism of post-War Poland, he plunged early into political activism. At 15, he founded a revisionist discussion club; at 16, in what must be a record, he was personally denounced by the country's Communist leader, Wladyslaw Gomulka. At 18, he was arrested for the first time. Thirty-nine other occasions would follow.

A wave of virulent repression with strong anti-Semitic overtones crushed the student movement of 1968. When not in jail, Michnik spent the 1970s, along with his older friend and fellow dissident Jacek Kuroń, probing the possibilities for common civic action between intellectuals like themselves and the two main pillars of Polish society – the working class and the Catholic Church. A key moment came in 1976 when Michnik and his colleagues formed the Workers' Defence Committee (KOR) to assist those who had been arrested for protesting against price increases.

In neighbouring Czechoslovakia, the dissident playwright Vaclav Havel had begun formulating the philosophy of non-violent resistance that he would champion in his famous essay "The Power of the Powerless." Influenced by the writings of the exiled political philosopher Leszek Kolakowski, Michnik was developing something similar in Poland. In August 1978, Michnik, Kuroń, and Havel were among a handful of Polish, Czech, and Slovak dissidents who slipped their police watchers to meet up in the mountains bordering their two countries for an afternoon of toasts and intellectual discussion. Michnik helped arrange the smuggling of Havel's essay to Warsaw, where it was published first in Polish.

The main idea behind "living within the truth," in Havel's phrase, and "living in dignity," in Kolakowski's, was to behave "as if" one were in a free country. Like the Soviet dissidents Andrei Sakharov and Alexander Solzhenitsyn, citizens should pretend that the "laws" announced by the country's rulers were real laws and demand that they respect them. The goal was to create a free public sphere to substitute for the one controlled by the authorities. Instead of complaining about censorship, citizens should publish their own books and newspapers. Rather than accept historical distortions, they should write and teach their own history. And, unlike the conspiratorial movements of the past, they should do all this openly and – where possible – invite their police handlers to the conversation.

In the summer of 1980, Michnik was vacationing in the mountains when revolution broke out. A strike in Gdansk by shipyard workers, angry at the lack of meat in the stores, metamorphosed into a massive uprising of citizens, 10 million of whom were soon members of the banned trade union Solidarity. This had little to do with the intellectuals of KOR. To Michnik, the strike leader Lech Wałęsa's project for an autonomous union seemed "extravagant and irresponsible." To his delight, he was proved wrong. Intellectuals, workers, and much of the rest of the population found themselves arm in arm.

After General Jaruzelski imposed martial law in December 1981, Michnik spent several years in jail. However, rather than silencing him, this turned Michnik into an international celebrity in human rights circles. From his prison cell, he managed to publish a stream of essays and open letters telling off his persecutors with a mixture of historical analogy and electrifying bravado. During his total of six years spent in Communist prisons, Michnik wrote five books.

By the late 1980s, the stalemate between generals and citizens was crumbling in the face of Gorbachev's new foreign policy. In 1989, the ruling party let Solidarity run in the first semi-free elections, and it defeated the Communist candidates in every seat it was allowed to contest in the Sejm, and all but one in the Senate. Michnik helped Wałęsa negotiate a transition with General Jaruzelski that peacefully transferred power to a new democratic leadership.

In some ways, the most remarkable part came afterwards. Unlike certain of his colleagues, Michnik discovered a vocation for reconciliation. His motives combined pragmatism – one could not, as in Brecht's famous couplet, "dissolve the people and elect a new one" – and an allergy to oversimplifications, whether historical or moral. As founding editor of the influential newspaper *Gazeta Wyborcza*, Michnik argued for historical memory combined with tolerance and dialogue: "Amnesty yes, Amnesia no!"

He made up with and forgave his former jailer, General Jaruzelski, accepting the general's view that martial law had saved Poland from the worse fate of a Soviet invasion. Michnik later recalled how, at Gorbachev's birthday party one year, the former Soviet leader was amused to see the two Poles walking "almost hand in hand." Gorbachev also earned Michnik's deep respect for allowing 1989 to unfold.

Michnik's refusal to entertain rancour leaves him sometimes isolated amid the Polish discourse of victimhood. Some fault him for his lack of Russophobia. He is, he likes to say, "an anti-Soviet Russophile," who can – and does – recite Mandelstam at the drop of a hat. He is inspired by the tradition of Russian liberals and freethinkers that reaches back from Sakharov to 19th century political writers such as Alexander Herzen.

Navalny is less known in the West. A few newspaper articles and magazine profiles have described his struggle against the Kremlin but left much unclear about his ideas. This book helps fill in the picture.

Born in 1976, he is from that borderline cohort of Russians who are old enough to remember life under Communism but young enough to have been formed by what came after. The son of an officer in the Soviet missile forces, Navalny spent his childhood on military bases. His grandmother, we learn here, was among the Soviet troops that captured the Reichstag in 1945.

He studied law and then took courses at Moscow's

Financial Academy. For some years, he worked at grass roots organising for Yabloko, one of the liberal political parties formed in the 1990s, and watched it dwindle away, undermined by a mixture of Kremlin harassment, its own ineffectiveness, and the low appeal of Putin critics in the years of rapid growth. After the party's leaders expelled Navalny for marching with some radical nationalists, he started to develop his own approach to poking at the increasingly authoritarian political system.

In 2007, he began to buy small numbers of shares in large state companies, and to turn up at their annual meetings to ask embarrassing questions. At Transneft, for instance, he insisted on knowing why the management would not reveal the recipients of the hundreds of millions of dollars of "charitable contributions" the company made each year. In a widely read blog, he exposed corrupt activities of the regime's insiders and heaped ridicule on the Kremlin's explanations.

Navalny's Anti-Corruption Foundation soon became a kind of incubator for online civic activism projects. One site, *Rosyama* ("Russian Pothole"), enables Russians to quickly and painlessly demand road repairs. After users photograph a hole in the road, the computer system generates a complaint to the relevant authorities. If the repair is not completed within the period prescribed by law, the website automatically produces a complaint to the prosecutors. All the user has to do is print out and mail the forms.

Another site, *Rospil* ("Russian Kickbacks"), exploits the regulation requiring all tenders for public contracts to be published online along with the winning bid. Navalny's volunteer lawyers seek out and post on the *Rospil* website details of tenders that seem designed to favour an insider.

Navalny's goal, he said, was to make it easy for everyone to spend "15 minutes a day struggling against the regime." He consciously imitates Amnesty International's strategy of providing members low cost ways to get involved, in AI's case by encouraging members to write letters to dictators about their political prisoners. One internet project offered a variety of small actions that sympathisers could take, to press for reform, from posting a flier in their entryway to making a donation.

While irritating to the Kremlin, such initiatives drew relatively little response at first. That changed after Navalny emerged as the charismatic figurehead of the 2011-12 mass protests. With Putin's return as president from May 2012, the authorities struck back. A series of new laws and regulations restricted demonstrations, and imposed a variety of penalties on opposition activism. Targeting Navalny, prosecutors charged that he had stolen a massive quantity of wood from a state lumber company while serving as adviser to the governor of Kirov Region. The case, which investigators had already dropped more than once for lack of evidence, seemed like a joke. But he was convicted in July 2013 and sentenced to five years in a labour camp. With bewildering speed, the authorities then decided to release him and allow him to run in that year's Moscow mayoral election, presumably to make the result seem legitimate. One Kremlin adviser I spoke to at the time gave him at most 15-17 percent of the vote. He won 27 percent, according to the official results, and maybe more in actuality.

As the protest movement dwindled in late 2012, the prosecutor produced a new case – this time against both Navalny and his brother Oleg, who ran a shipping company. The brothers were said to have embezzled about $1.8 million from their client, the beauty products company Yves Rocher, although the latter denied having suffered any loss. In December 2014, the judge found the brothers guilty and sentenced both to three and a half years in a labour camp along with large fines, but then suspended Alexei's sentence. Oleg Navalny is serving his term in Russia's Penal Colony Number 5 in Orel Region–a constant reminder to his brother of the costs of fighting the Kremlin.

In the face of this increasing pressure, Alexei has himself attempted to "live in dignity." Since February 2014, the authorities had placed him under house arrest, attaching an electronic monitoring bracelet to his ankle. Although Russian law does not permit continued house arrest after a defendant has been sentenced, no one removed the bracelet. So, taking matters into his own hands, Navalny cut it off, posted a picture of it online, and began walking around the city at will. The police officers assigned to trail him at first pleaded with him to return home. After a few weeks, they stopped following. The Kremlin seems unsure what to do about this 39-year-old who won 630,000 votes in Moscow's 2013 election and whose YouTube videos about corrupt officials can quickly attract 4 million viewers.

Moscow liberals often scold Navalny for his nationalism. In 2006, violence broke out between Chechens and ethnic Russians in the Karelian city of Kondopoga. The next year, Navalny joined with two others to found a "nationalist-democratic" movement called *Narod* ("The People"). Its manifesto called for honest elections and checks and balances, and denounced provocateurs that preached xenophobia and violence against non-natives. It also demanded the legalisation of handguns and the deportation of immigrants who did not respect Russia's "law and traditions."

The conversations presented here should clarify the nature of Navalny's nationalism today. He comes across as a moderate, European-style conservative. He believes that Russia should introduce the kind of visa regime and work quotas that most Western countries have used for years to manage labour migration. He would like the Orthodox

Church to cultivate a respect for tradition, family values, and Christian teaching, but to stay out of politics.

Rather than shunning Russians with nationalist or conservative views, he argues for engaging them in dialogue. Instead of allowing such people to drift towards extremism, he urges efforts to win them over to a kind of "civic nationalism predicated not on physiology or a sense of national superiority but on universal civil rights and freedoms, on the potential to determine the fate of our country together." This civic nationalism does not reject minorities: it embraces them. And some well-known Russian liberals of minority ethnicity or religion – such as the economist Sergei Guriev and the journalist Yevgenia Albats – are among Navalny's strongest supporters.

At first sight, these two fighters for civic and political freedom look quite different. They come from different countries, generations, and parts of the political spectrum. While Michnik started out an idealistic leftist seeking to replace Stalinism with a humanist socialism, Navalny began in the 1990s, by his own account, a "market fundamentalist." They struggle against different models of illiberal regime. Michnik's adversary was a Communist party dictatorship, controlled by a distant colonial superpower. Navalny faces a personalised pseudo-democracy with market economics, a determination to crush independent opposition, and little ideology beyond sulky anti-Westernism.

A huge gap separates the technologies of resistance of the 1970s Communist world from those of the current information age. Where Michnik had carbon-paper *samizdat*, Navalny today has Facebook and Twitter. Solidarity spread its message by means of the "Flying University" – a series of flash seminars held in sympathisers' apartments; the Russian oppositionists use blogs and internet campaigns.

In temperament, both men are gregarious, but Michnik is

an enthusiast, Navalny more of an ironist. Michnik was determined to avoid being pressed into politics. Navalny hungrily seeks an opening. Most of Michnik's Russian friends are the type of unworldly dissidents that Navalny says he used to think of as the "neighbourhood crazies." Navalny's associates bristle with IT skills and modern knowhow.

Indeed, Navalny – who a few years ago engaged an *HR-schick* (human resources specialist) to find him a press secretary – exudes a kind of problem-solving, corporate dynamism. He fights corruption with a whiteboard, flowcharts, and company statements, and is probably the only revolutionary who can claim a publication in the *Harvard Business Review* (Russian edition).

While the Michnik story has a beginning and a middle, although –thankfully – not yet an end, Navalny's is a work in progress, an early draft. His key challenges lie ahead.

They disagree about some things – in particular, the 1990s. Navalny, perhaps punishing himself for past idealism, sees the decade as a betrayal. At the time, he cheered Yeltsin's shelling of the parliament in October 1993 in the face of an armed uprising of ultranationalists and Communists. Now he views it as a mistake. He sees the 1996 election as a fraud. Michnik seems less sure that, had the ultranationalists or Communists prevailed, they would have agreed to hand power back later on.

More aggravating even than corruption for Navalny is hypocrisy. He reserves his greatest scorn not for Putin but for Anatoli Chubais, the architect of 1990s privatisation, who now heads a state company and stays quiet about the faults of his boss. Navalny seems to blame Yeltsin for Putin almost more than he blames Putin himself. Even when he agrees with the main point, one feels Michnik at times resisting the younger activist's generalised rhetoric, the tone of denunciation.

And yet, despite obvious differences, the striking thing

is how much these two men have in common. Both have shown the courage to face imprisonment for their beliefs. (While Michnik spent six years behind bars, Navalny's street protests have landed him in detention for several two-week spells as well as under house arrest for months.) Each has found the endurance to withstand the daily grind of petty persecution, to survive the enervating ambiguities and slippery slopes of the dissident's life.

Both seem a little surprised by how often they agree, including on issues where Poles and Russians might be expected to have different perspectives. There is only one route to European modernity (no country has a "special path"). Judicial reform should be the first priority. Lustration must be a matter of court investigations, not politicised reckonings. Democracy and a free press are the only cures for corruption. A legitimate referendum in Crimea will be the only way to resolve that region's status. They even concur – and this may surprise some Western readers – in their disapproval of Pussy Riot's performance in Moscow's Cathedral of Christ the Saviour, although they also both consider the punishment as excessive.

What can Poland's history of transition teach Russians eager for a more democratic political order? At first, the comparison seems discouraging. If we equate 1968 in Poland to 2011 in Russia, a long path lies ahead before Russia's dissidents get to their round table talks. Moreover, Michnik insists that Poland's breakthrough depended on a certain individual: it could not have occurred had Mikhail Gorbachev not made the courageous choice to "open the door." The Putin regime seems determined to keep all doors, windows, and air vents nailed shut.

Yet history, when it repeats itself, often does so in a new tempo. Changes that required a generation in one country sometimes take only years in others. And Russia today, unlike Poland before 1989, is not under the diktat of an external power. So the constraints on change may not be comparable.

Michnik's tone is never didactic, but one can detach some lessons from the discussion. The first is to beware of revolutions. In another recent work, Michnik quotes Danton: "In revolutions, power remains at the end with the biggest scoundrels!" If Solidarity was a revolution, it was a self-limiting one. The Polish dissidents knew they could not prevail against Soviet tanks with sticks and stones. By remaining non-violent, they also avoided the emergence of their own Jacobins.

Yet, if one should not force the pace with violence, the second lesson is to be ready when power falls into one's lap. The scale of Solidarity's victory in 1989, which came after several waves of mobilisation and repression, took the movement's leaders by surprise. When a representative of the Communist old guard consulted Michnik about a transition, it seemed to him at first "some fantasy or absurdist scenario." He "just hadn't grasped that they could possibly accept their absolute trouncing!" Michnik had to argue with other Solidarity leaders who wanted to stay in opposition and criticise from the sidelines.

A third point Michnik emphasises is the danger of trusting secret police files. Instead, one should view these as sources of rumours and lies rather than of unbiased information. If it is not to poison the transition, lustration must be handled carefully, within the framework of a judicial procedure, and not in a political forum or by some ad hoc populist tribunal.

And, finally, the most important lesson is the need for intellectual activists to forge connections to the mass of the population. In Poland, that meant joining forces with factory workers and the Church. In Russia, the great challenge

Navalny faces is to find common language with the people of Russia's provinces, the ones who do not read his blog or even know his name.

In Poland, KOR and then Solidarity emerged when the dissidents began to help workers in their economic battles, and defend them when they too were targeted by the state's apparatus of repression. Rather than seeking to persuade ordinary people to share the activists' concerns, the activists learned the concerns of ordinary people and helped in their pursuit. Faced with economic grievances, authoritarian regimes have a counterproductive habit of turning them into political ones. Thus, opposition to the Communists converged, while support for the old regime dissipated.

The effectiveness of Navalny's efforts to push Russia toward a freer political order remains to be seen. Will the community formed in Moscow's snow-covered squares four years ago reappear, perhaps in a new configuration? There are no guarantees. Those in the Kremlin are determined to prevent this, and the patriotic upsurge over Crimea's annexation has changed the focus, at least for the moment. The return to power of Poland's illiberal Law and Justice Party in October 2015 suggests that Michnik's work may also not be over. Meanwhile, this book offers an inspiring view of two dedicated fighters for civic and political freedom engaging with the key questions that confront such activists in authoritarian states around the world.

Introduction
Alexei Navalny

The isolation in which Russia has today found itself is to the detriment of all and sundry. At such times it is of particular importance to maintain a dialogue with the outside world. I feel lucky to have had the opportunity to converse with an individual uniquely experienced not only in battling an authoritarian regime, but in building a new country on genuinely democratic foundations. Adam Michnik is a living legend. A human rights activist, oppositionist and political prisoner, he succeeded, together with his colleagues from Solidarity, in dismantling the old regime without bloodshed, while also creating the most widely read socio-political newspaper in the newly-free Poland. Of particular significance for me is the following: Adam's entire existence is testament to the fact that it is possible to "live not by lies," and that the only way to defeat a dictatorship is to preserve one's inner freedom, even when no other freedoms remain. He was one of the few who dared to dream about a Europe-oriented future for his country during a desolate and stagnant epoch, when even the staunchest optimists thought it inevitable that their present condition would stretch on into infinity. Michnik's dream became reality. Our three-day conversation has demonstrated that, for all of Russia's uniqueness, the challenges it is currently facing are not at all as unique as we've come to believe. The path we must follow has been trodden by many Eastern-bloc countries; they have succeeded, and so too shall we; I'm more convinced of this than ever before. We shall succeed if we learn to be "free people in an unfree country" – something Adam Michnik himself learned to be, and taught others to be.

Moscow, August 2015

Introduction
Adam Michnik

My conversations with Alexei Navalny have proved an important, stimulating experience. I'm grateful to my Russian colleagues for making our encounter happen. Alexei has turned out to be an unhackneyed interlocutor. You can disagree with what he has to say, but it's impossible to ignore him. His voice is the voice of the "other" Russia. The Russia that all too rarely captures the attention of the outside world, overly preoccupied with its Kremlinological pursuits; the Russia looked upon with hope by friends and allies, including yours truly – an anti-Soviet Russophile.

I've always admired the Russia of the human rights activists who had enough courage to throw down the gauntlet to Brezhnev, Andropov and Suslov. I became acquainted with that Russia through the works of Sakharov and Solzhenitsyn, Sinyavsky and Daniel, Bukovsky and Amalrik. I strove to gulp down the air of hope wafting through the songs of Okudzhava, Vysotsky and Galich, circulating through the poetry of Akhmatova, Brodsky and Mandelstam. It seemed to many back then that there was no Russia other than the Russia of the executioners. I, for my part, always knew there were two Russias: the Russia of hangmen, and that of hanged men. I've always admired the Russia of freedom-loving rebels and despised the Russia of executioners (just as I despise the executioners of all countries and peoples, not excluding the Polish variety).

Russia is a country of extraordinary people, people worthy of respect and admiration. Some have blessed me with their friendship – one of my life's genuine treasures. My friendships with Sergei Kovalyov, Lyudmila Alexeyeva, Viktor Shenderovich, Lilia Shevtsova, Boris Nemtsov, Grigory Yavlinsky, Andrei Zubov, and many others have served to reinforce my belief in the good sense of that old Polish slogan, "For our freedom and yours." Because freedom is undividable. And if my Russian friends are being denied their freedom, I feel humiliated and deprived of freedom myself.

Many people today are anxiously looking on at a Russia that has annexed Crimea, fomented unrest in the Donbas … We're alarmed by the bellicose thrust of the mendacious propaganda campaigns, by the clampdown on Russian democrats. Our hope lies in the democratic opposition; only through it can this wonderful country be rescued from the catastrophe that the Kremlin's policy of both cold and "hot" war against the entire world is threatening to bring about. Every one of my Russian friends basely accused of treason by the regime should repeat the words of the great Russian philosopher Pyotr Chaadaev: "Believe me, I love my country more than any of you, I wish her glory, I'm not blind to the great qualities of my people … I didn't learn to love my country with eyes shut, head bowed, lips closed. I find that a man can be of use to his country only if he understands her well; I believe the time of blind adoration has passed, that we now owe our Motherland the truth above all else … I confess that I'm a stranger to this blithe, lazy patriotism, which contrives to see everything in a rosy light, pampers its own illusions, and which, lamentably, has afflicted many of our good minds today."

I'm sure Alexei Navalny would subscribe to these words as well. He has already done much for the cause of democracy in Russia, and I'm convinced he will do yet more. I shall repeat the words Bulgakov's Woland addresses to Margarita: "Everything will be as it should; that's what the world is built on." What a truly great writer he was!

Warsaw, August 2015

1

From Dissidents to Solidarity

Navalny Pan Adam, I suggest we begin with the history of the Polish opposition movement. How did you come to be involved with the ten-million-strong Solidarity organisation? As I understand it, 1968 was, in a sense, a landmark year for you: the Soviet invasion of Czechoslovakia dispelled any lingering hopes that the system could be reformed from above, without pressure from below. Even today, many people in Russia remain convinced that to obtain change you need only wait for certain "systemic liberals" to prevail in the battle of the political elites – no social activism or pressure on the authorities required, change will simply materialise of its own accord. You've experienced this first-hand yourself, have you not?

Michnik Despite the "thaw" of 1956,[1] there was no opposition in Poland in the usual sense of the word. There were people with liberal views, but they weren't organised. There were groups of like-minded friends. In 1964, a group of writers penned an open letter against censorship. The following year, Jacek Kuroń and Karol Modzelewski wrote their *Open Letter to the Party*, in which they analysed what was happening in the country from a Marxist perspective, channelling Milovan Djilas' idea of the party *nomenklatura* as a "new class" that had usurped power. They were arrested and sentenced to three and three-and-a-half years in prison respectively. They were the first to speak openly of the inhumanity of the system, and expressed no remorse during the course of their trial. Their discourse was, of course, still trapped in the snares of Marxist-Leninist language, but it had now assumed an anti-state character. The trial catalysed the university movement. Students came to meetings, organised debates, asked inconvenient questions: Why had Khrushchev's report to the 20th Party Congress[2] remained unpublished? What happened in Katyn?[3] What was the nature of the Molotov-Ribbentrop Pact?[4] Party figures dubbed these students "commandos."

With this intellectual baggage in hand, we arrived in 1968. At the start of that year, the Party had made the great mistake of labelling as "anti-Soviet," and banning a performance of Adam Mickiewicz's poetic drama *Dzyady* [*Forefathers' Eve*] at the National Theatre. The final performance was attended by students who staged a demonstration against censorship. The university authorities decided to expel two students from Warsaw University as a warning to the rest. Those students were Henryk Szlajfer and myself. And all this was accompanied by anti-Semitic rhetoric: Zionists, apparently, were destabilising the situation in the country. It was then that our "commandos" decided that, as Okudzhava had once sung, they must "join hands so as not to perish one by one." A student rally was organised for March 8. To our surprise, students from other universities across the country joined Warsaw students in a solidarity rally only a few days later. Student demonstrations began in Krakow, Poznan and other university centres. We were arrested, but, just like Kuroń and Karol Modzelewski, we expressed no remorse. We were, of course, inspired by the Prague Spring[5] – if such things could happen in Czechoslovakia, we thought, then they could happen in Poland as well.

Wladyslaw Gomulka, First Secretary of the Polish United Workers' Party, adopted a very uncompromising stance. He was ready for bloodshed. He'd found himself in a difficult situation:

within the party, he was opposed by a group of national chauvinists[6] that had emerged during the 1967 Six Day War in the Middle East.[7] They unleashed a terrible anti-Semitic campaign, directed against the intelligentsia, which swept Poland. The Kremlin proceeded to make it clear that Tito and Ceauşescu were quite enough already, and that it wouldn't tolerate the coming to power of any Polish nationalists. Gomulka managed to cling on to power. But it was then that we realised that the road towards liberalisation was not the only one the party could take – it could also go down the road of chauvinistic nationalism, bolstered by mistrust of Germans and Jews.

After a very eventful 1968, absolute stagnation set in. Gomulka did, I believe, achieve a significant success in the international arena: West German Chancellor Willy Brandt recognised the inviolability of Poland's western border.[8] But this meant nothing for the wider population. Brandt signed the papers on 7th December, 1970, and by the 12th the price of meat, butter and other products had already been hiked up, triggering a serious wave of worker protests in Gdansk. After being released from prison (I'd served out a year and a half), I worked at a factory; and met the December unrest as a simple proletarian. The practical outcomes of this protest weren't extensive. Gomulka was replaced by the moderate Edward Gierek, but that's about as far as it went. The reason for this, I think, was the absence of political slogans. The intelligentsia didn't get involved in the movement – the purges of 1968 had wrung its neck. After December's unrest, we turned our gaze in the direction of Russia, home to the opposition titans Solzhenitsyn and Sakharov …

Navalny How did you come to know about them?

Michnik Anybody with an interest in politics knew about these people. We read their books, which were published in Paris.

Everyone knew about the existence in Russia of *samizdat,* which did not yet exist in Poland. And we were ashamed. We had emigrants too, and those who weren't afraid could publish their works under a pseudonym. But the country was still ruled by fear. We read a letter penned by Moscow-based writers in defence of Andrei Sinyavsky and Yuli Daniel[9] – a very carefully worded letter, but one with a manifestly oppositionist stance. The letter was signed by household names such as Ehrenburg, Okudzhava, Akhmadulina, Chukovsky and others. It became clear that a conflict between the intelligentsia and the party had come to a head, and it manifested itself as a struggle for human rights. At the same time, representatives of various social strata – the intelligentsia, the church, students, and, ultimately, workers – entered the fray against the party as well.

Navalny And did the Polish party elite itself sense the discontent brewing in society? Did they take any steps to accommodate the opposition?

Michnik After the crushing of the Prague Spring, they were too afraid of the Soviet Union and, indeed, of Polish society itself. They understood only too well that the situation was taking a turn for the worse. The new party leadership opted for a strategy of economic bribery: thanks to Western and Soviet loans, they managed to maintain relatively acceptable standards of living, as well as making it easier to work abroad – and even allowing Pepsi Cola into the country.

In the early 1970s, talk began about the need to accord the Communist party the status of a constitutional institution. This idea, I believe, came from Moscow. The opposition had not yet managed to consolidate, but an open letter was penned in protest against such constitutional changes. You ask whether there was hope for change from the top? No, there was not; after 1968 and Czechoslovakia we no longer entertained any illusions about the possibility of reform from above. If General Secretary Dubček and his team had failed to achieve anything, *we* certainly stood no chance of changing things.

Navalny Given the situation that had arisen, the Polish party leadership could have used the student and worker unrest as a tool for bargaining with Moscow, secretly supporting your group in the meantime. But this isn't something they went in for, is it?

Michnik For our Communists, this was an alien concept.

Navalny If we regard the situation as a confrontation between colony and parent state, then, in theory, the Communists should have all felt themselves *Polish* – above and beyond anything else – and therefore sympathised with the students ...

Michnik Firstly, your average Polish communist feared the Russians. Secondly, most of the party leaders believed that it was *Stalin* who'd given them power, and that he'd also given Poland its new western border.

Navalny So great was the fear of Germany?

Michnik Indeed. This was a generation whose memories of Hitler and the Nazi occupation were only too vivid. Gierek was perceived by many as a perfectly satisfactory figure – a Polish patriot whose endeavours shouldn't be interfered with. Similar sentiments were widespread in the Polish episcopate. I remember our conversations with Cardinal Wyszyński. Everyone was afraid of Soviet intervention; this thought was a recurring theme.

In 1976, the government hiked prices up once again, triggering a wave of protests across the country. Gierek didn't dare resort to tough measures; yes, there were arrests, but the custodial sentences that followed generally only lasted days, or months at most. It was then that we organised the Workers' Defence Committee [*Komitet Obrony Robotników*, hereafter KOR], and it was the wisest decision we could have taken. Most of the protesters were workers. In June 1976, the government backtracked, lowering prices again, but many people involved in the unfolding events – ordinary workers – landed up in prison. These workers are in jail, we said, we have to support and protect them. Intelligence regarding this state of affairs was immediately disseminated across the entire country. Thus was born the Polish human rights movement. And here's the most important thing: we believed that no reforms, no impetus for change, would be forthcoming from the government; our task was not to reform the regime, but to protect ourselves from it. Young activists engaged with workers, KOR personnel materialised at the shipyard in Gdansk, at the Ursus tractor factory, and so forth. We came armed with the idea of creating free, not state-sponsored, trade unions. Except for a group of activists, there was nothing in place, yet a new mythology was being forged.

Navalny How was this "mythology" disseminated? Did you already have your own underground presses?

Michnik Our *samizdat* was in its infancy at the time. A fresh edition of our magazine *Rabotnik* [*Worker*] would typically be published once a month. And, of course, there was Radio Free Europe.[10] We could reach out to 10,000-15,000 people via *samizdat*, while radio allowed us to address millions!

Navalny Radio broadcasts weren't jammed, as was the case in the Soviet Union?

Michnik. They were – but with the same laughable success.

Navalny And how old were your fellow-thinkers?

Michnik These were people of different generations. I was 30 years old; Jacek Kuroń was 42. The celebrated writer Jerzy Andrzejewski, author of the novel *Ashes and Diamonds*, was 67. These people served as embodiments of the movement, but in practice it was primarily made up of young people aged 22 to 30.

Navalny So the KOR began to destroy the state's monopoly over the social sphere, and people, joining forces of their own accord, began to create a human rights movement. If the regime hadn't jailed these people, would all these processes have got under way later?

Michnik Perhaps. But all of us realised then that this was only the beginning, and that we needed to take things forward. And so we created the Flying University.[11] We began inviting students to political history lectures and teaching them economics and literature without clogging their brains with lies and propaganda.

Navalny And what was the regime's response?

Michnik They tried throwing spanners in the works. We'd get visits from state security personnel. But they didn't know what to do.

Wladyslaw Bartoszewski – a great patriot, an Auschwitz prisoner, and subsequently an inmate of a Stalinist prison in Poland – passed away not so long ago. Now he, for example, would tell his audience about anti-Hitler conspiracies. How can you arrest a man just because he's telling young people about the fight against Hitler! Gierek knew that if he wanted Western money and prestige, he couldn't arrest Bartoszewski. And he didn't arrest him.

Navalny Yet the power of Western influence was considerable ...

Michnik It certainly was. Now I think that Putin's facing the same dilemma. His image in the West has been almost completely tarnished in the wake of events in Ukraine. But he really doesn't want to become a pariah. In this sense, a parallel can be drawn between Putin and Gierek.

Navalny Did you maintain ties with the Polish émigré community?

Michnik Of course. Without it, we wouldn't have enjoyed such support – political as much as financial – in the West. There were emigrants working for the Polish division of Radio Free Europe. During my stay in Paris in 1976-1977, I made the acquaintance of Russian emigrants, too: Vladimir Bukovsky, Natalia Gorbanevskaya, Vladimir Maksimov, Andrei Sinyavsky, Viktor Nekrasov, Alexander Galich. Russian authors were extensively featured in Polish *samizdat* publications. Natalia Gorbanevskaya, who knew Polish very well indeed, was practically an icon in Poland.

2

Battling the Regime

Navalny Am I right in thinking that the KOR effectively adopted the slogan "Respect the Constitution," used by Soviet dissidents and human rights defenders?

Michnik They did.

Navalny And that in its early years the movement was small, in terms of number of participants?

Michnik That's right.

Navalny How did you manage to transform the modestly-sized KOR into the ten-million-strong Solidarity movement?

Michnik It was a miracle. The summer of 1980 saw a simmering of social unrest. I'd been planning to go to the Tatra Mountains with my girlfriend. Jacek Kuroń called me up and said, "Adam, this is a historic moment!" I replied, "Jacek, you've been telling me the same thing for the past twenty years! I want to go off to the mountains with my girlfriend!" Turned out he was right, though.

It all started with the Moscow Olympic Games, where the Soviet regime was showing off Communism.[12] Moscow needed a lot of meat – meat that was exported from Poland. We, meanwhile, could only get produce using our ration cards – there wasn't any meat in the shops. Railway workers began blocking the freight trains.

Navalny What were their demands? What exactly did they want?

Michnik They wanted the shops to be stocked with meat. Their demands were purely economic. Then the workers went on strike in Lublin. In August, a strike led by KOR activists began at the Lenin Shipyard in Gdansk. The activists gave the protest a political colouring from the word go, calling for the establishment of free and independent trade unions. This represented a total de-legitimisation of the Communist regime, and of the so-called "dictatorship of the proletariat;" the proletariat itself was saying "enough!" to the regime! The government was hoping until the very end that it'd be able to buy the workers' cooperation, but it got a firm *No* in response, because the protests were being spearheaded by representatives of the democratic opposition. And when ordinary people across the country realised how serious the Gdansk protest actually was, all of Poland stood up to back it. The authorities were forced to make concessions, and bowed to our demands regarding the legalisation of independent trade unions. A workers' protest of this scale had never occurred in the history of the country. The whole world was still speaking the language of Marxism, the language of the working class. And now that very same working class (not the bourgeoisie, not the intelligentsia!) had rebelled against the Communist Party!

Navalny So Solidarity acquired its ten-million-strong contingent as early as that August? When did the actual word "Solidarity" enter the scene? And when did people start identifying with the movement?

Michnik It was after we signed the agreements with the government to secure the right to free trade unions. A dilemma arose: should we create a single large trade union or lots of small independent ones? People from the regions were saying a single union was the way to go, otherwise we'd all be snuffed out one by one. Karol Modzelewski suggested calling the single trade union Solidarity. And then it became obvious that something completely new was in the offing. The Communists thought they could just replicate the scenario that had unfurled after the war. In the early post-war years, Poland still had a political opposition and a free press; the Communists used "salami tactics" against them – exploiting their disunity and numerical weakness, they eliminated one organisation after another as though they were slicing their way through a sausage.[13] So now they were expecting a multitude of independent trade unions that would be easy to deal with. But times had changed. New people were heading the movement, and we managed to maintain a united front.

Navalny In its earliest stages, the movement was positioned as having a socialist underpinning. Did you genuinely still believe in socialism or was this a sort of mimicry, an attempt to integrate yourselves into existing canonical structures? Or was the movement originally non-ideological? Or anti-colonial, perhaps?

Michnik It was a movement against one-party dictatorship. We were taking a stand against the privileges enjoyed by the *nomenklatura* [bureaucracy] and state security personnel. We were speaking out for human rights, clamouring for free trade unions, and calling for the erection of a monument in honour of the workers killed in December 1970 in Gdansk.[14] We had no anti-Soviet slogans and spoke very cautiously about the Soviet Union; everyone was afraid of making brazen proclamations. The memory of Hungary, Czechoslovakia and Afghanistan were all too fresh in our minds. As for socialism, we didn't declare ourselves opposed to it; but by that time no one believed that socialism was possible unless it came without a one-party system and state security structures. The dictatorship of the Communist party had discredited the very idea of socialism.

No one fully understood what it was we should actually *want*, other than democratic rights. But we understood perfectly well what we *did not* want.

Navalny That's an interesting situation. You were afraid that Brezhnev might send troops in, while Brezhnev – his hands tied by Afghanistan – was afraid he'd have to do just that.

Michnik Yes. It would have been better for Moscow if Jaruzelski had brought the situation under control himself. But for Poland, too, Jaruzelski represented a better option than Soviet intervention. Brezhnev couldn't afford to lose Poland – we're talking the heart of Europe here. Withdrawing troops from Albania, Romania or Afghanistan was a possibility; withdrawing them from Poland wasn't. You're absolutely right in saying he was afraid. No one in the Kremlin trusted the Poles. They all remembered our rebuffing of Tukhachevsky, Stalin and Budyonny in 1920.[15] But no one expected the emergence of the ten-million-strong Solidarity, which transformed all our preconceptions regarding the essence of communism.

Navalny In modern Russia, the independent trade union movement is very restricted in scope and prefers to limit itself to social slogans while keeping its distance from politics. But political slogans immediately took centre-stage in Poland ...

Michnik Indeed. Political ideas were right at the forefront of things – they embodied the very nature of the movement. But today everything is different. Trade unions today no longer care to engage with politics.

Navalny In December 1981, General Wojciech Jaruzelski mounted a coup d'état, declared martial law and detained thousands of Solidarity activists. The question – and it's one we're very interested in, for obvious reasons – is this: how did the movement survive in such repressive conditions?

Michnik This was martial rule "with a human face."[16] People weren't killed or shot, and political activists were soon granted amnesty. Only the most 'dangerous' leaders were imprisoned: Kuroń, Modzelevsky, Gwiazda, and myself. And, crucially, we enjoyed society's support. Poland witnessed virtually no instance of Stalinist terror; given an order from above, people weren't morally ready to accost political opponents of the regime and shout, "Wałęsa is an enemy of the people!" We felt public support. After the introduction of martial law, everyone had lost all respect for the regime and its ideology. That was the absolute end. When martial law began, it became almost fashionable to pin a power resistor to your blazer or jumper as a symbol of defiance. Workers would turn up at their factories with Solidarity badges. Symbols of the movement were everywhere, and particularly in churches. Cultural figures refused to make television appearances on the grounds that this was unseemly behaviour. And those who continued to make them, hardly felt great about doing so – it meant they were kowtowing to the regime. Mikhalkov is now behaving in a similar way in Russia, but he feels just dandy about it. We had different sorts of people, though – the famous actress Maja Komorowska, for example. She didn't appear on television, but came to speak in churches. Some people turned in their party cards by way of protest.

Navalny So before martial law was introduced, many people were afraid to openly express their views, but this fear disappeared after its introduction? That's a very paradoxical thing.

Michnik It *is* paradoxical, I agree. The Catholic Church played an enormous role.[17] It became a haven for the opposition. There were lots of different bishops, of course: some openly supported the opposition, others acted with extreme caution. But the Church, as the lifeblood of the nation, had always been opposed to communist violence. And what's more, the pope was a Pole; we'd known him back in his Krakow days. John Paul II[18] didn't fully understand the capitalist West, but he understood the communist East perfectly. He called for the renunciation of violence and hatred, and impelled us towards dialogue.

Three miracles served to foster a particular climate in society: the election of a Polish pope in 1978, the birth of Solidarity in 1980, and Czeslaw Milosz's Nobel Prize win that same year.

Navalny Among the priests who expressed support for Solidarity was one Jerzy Popieluszko,[19] assassinated by state security agents in 1984. Speaking on Echo Moscow [radio station] in the immediate aftermath of the murder of Boris Nemtsov, Waclaw Radziwinowicz, your newspaper's chief Russian correspondent, drew parallels between the two events.[20] How justified do you believe such parallels to be?

Michnik There are indeed parallels, I think. In the days following Popieluszko's murder, I was convinced that our generals were responsible, and I said as much in an interview with the French press. But I then came to see that this wasn't the case. For the first time in the history of communism, state security agency assassins had been put on public trial. We still don't know who exactly was behind the murder, but I believe it was Miroslaw Milewski, who oversaw the work of security agencies in the party politburo, and who maintained close links with Moscow. In 1991, in Moscow, I asked Oleg Kalugin what had happened to Popieluszko. "It wasn't us," he said. "We had this good mate, Miroslaw Milewski, in the Polish politburo, and he was the one behind the murder." I can't vouch for the veracity of the information. I believe that the killing of Popieluszko was necessary to instigate a radicalisation of the internal conflict in Poland. Hardliners were doing their best to push Jaruzelski into taking out the opposition. And I believe that if Putin was behind the murder of Nemtsov, everything would have been done differently, in a less brazen, less impudent fashion, rather than a stone's throw from the Kremlin, for all the world to see. I believe it was done to show Putin that he's no longer the top dog in Russia, as he was before.

Navalny Yes, going on the available evidence, the two scenarios definitely are similar. To all appearances, the man behind Nemtsov's murder is Ramzan Kadyrov. I think the situation could have developed in one of two ways. Putin might have praised Kadyrov for his struggle against the "fifth column," and Kadyrov might have interpreted this as an incentive to commit murder. Alternatively, certain people may be attempting to push Putin into taking more decisive action against the opposition. The latter scenario's more comparable to what happened in Poland.

Michnik And it seems more convincing to me. At the moment, Putin's policy is still not fully clear: he hasn't unleashed a witch hunt in the public sphere, nor has he declared Nemtsov an "enemy of the people." People with great power often wield no real power at all. Too many factors are determined by the prevailing environment.

Navalny What ramifications did the murder of Jerzy Popieluszko have on society at large?

Michnik It resulted in an absolute defeat for the regime. Up to a million people attended his funeral. Popieluszko was one of the symbols of the opposition; he made unmistakably oppositionist sermons in the centre of the capital. What's more, he had very close links with the opposition-minded intelligentsia, which was incredibly fond of him, despite consisting primarily of atheists. He was a simple, humble man, who had exerted influence on Warsaw's steelworkers. Workers who'd joined Solidarity were among his entourage. I knew him personally, though not too well. We weren't acquainted prior to the introduction of martial law. But when we were released from jail in 1984, all of us ex-prisoners attended a church service. Taking Jacek [Kuroń] and myself by the hand, he made his way through the crowd. A brave gesture on his part – we were being showcased as the nation's biggest enemies at the time. But he wasn't afraid to do it. He had a few problems with our Cardinal Jozef Glemp, and they were even planning to send him abroad on church matters.

At his funeral, Lech Wałęsa said, "Solidarity lives on, and will continue to live on, because you've laid down your life for it." Hearing that was like an electric shock, as if a jolt of electricity had surged through the million-strong crowd. And it became apparent then that Solidarity was alive and kicking.

Navalny Did the murder not result in the radicalisation of the opposition? Such a key event must surely have diminished the number of moderates in its ranks.

Michnik Yes, that did happen. But the radicals had no programme. We would have rather let the regime turn its back on dialogue than do it ourselves. In 1984, though, none of us believed that dialogue was possible. November 1984 saw the funeral of Jerzy Popieluszko, and in February '85 I was re-arrested and sentenced to two-and-a-half years in prison. They didn't so much as let me open my mouth during the trial.

Navalny You couldn't even make a closing statement?

Michnik I managed to get out a single sentence: "I forgive my detractors and castigators." The judge didn't appreciate the irony and simply replied with a "thank you."
Then came Gorbachev's *perestroika*.[21] Our opposition radicals doubted the veracity of the new Soviet leadership's alleged intentions, arguing that it was all deception and lies. They'd ask me whether I trusted Gorbachev. Good question, I'd reply, but you should really be asking his wife that. I was interested in what he was actually *doing*. Later, Yuri Levada, Viktor Sheinis and Natan Eidelman visited Warsaw, and they expressed their views without any regard for censorship, which meant that things really must've begun to change in Moscow. And so we started waiting for something fresh to happen.

Navalny How did you manage to coax the regime to the negotiating table?

Michnik We organised a so-called "gathering of the sixty:"

Bronislaw Geremek arranged public discussions on current topics, and Lech Wałęsa invited intellectuals, writers and scientists along to them. We planned to involve representatives from all spheres of public life – a total of sixty people.

We were willing to negotiate, but the government didn't want to hold talks with Solidarity as a whole, only with us as individuals. Zbigniew Brzezinski came over to Warsaw, I remember, and he was surprised we weren't agreeing to their terms. But our strength lay in our solidarity. Individual figures represented themselves, but Solidarity represented society at large. We were very well clued up on their Bolshevik tricks and firmly insisted on our terms.

Navalny Did the church continue to support you?

Michnik Not across the board. Cardinal Glemp wanted there to be special representation for Catholics. We refused – there was room for everybody in Solidarity, whether Catholics, Protestants or atheists. We were all united by our love of freedom. We echoed the Pope in proclaiming it impossible to carry out positive reforms for Catholics only. The Cardinal didn't agree with us.

3

Solidarity comes to Power

Navalny How did you manage to overcome the wrangling within the opposition camp?

Michnik A terrible economic crisis broke out in 1988. You can't imagine how bad it all was. The situation was much better in Russia. Poles would go over to the USSR to stock up on various goods. In Poland, there was a very strong general sense that the communist system was in its death throes. A new wave of strikes began under the slogan "There's no freedom without Solidarity." Our opponents realised that nothing would be possible without Wałęsa. They were prepared to stomach dealing with him – a worker, a Catholic, a paterfamilias – but they didn't want to deal with "gangsters" like Kuroń and Michnik. Wałęsa, though, wasn't going to sit down at the negotiating table without us. I told Lech that perhaps we needed to make concessions in this regard, but Wałęsa replied, "Adam, this isn't about you and it's not about Jacek – it's about them trying to pick my pocket straight away, and that just won't do." Later, the Communists realised that time was against them. So came the first televised debate between Wałęsa and Alfred Miodowicz, a Communist trade union representative. I advised Wałęsa to adopt a Gorbachevian rhetoric. "They're saying in Moscow that the end of the Stalinist system is nigh," he thundered on live TV. "What're *you* playing at in the meantime?" It was a real "you had to be there" moment.

The catastrophe happened live on air – the Communists were totally confounded! In August Wałęsa met with Interior Minister General Czeslaw Kiszczak. That was a significant juncture, marking the end of the strike while paving the way for dialogue. We were afraid they'd deceive us, but they'd now entered into the logic of dialogue.

Navalny Were there Solidarity supporters within the party-state apparatus?

Michnik Yes, of course.

Navalny How senior were they?

Michnik Andrzej Werblan, one of the party's main ideologists, was among them, for instance. Then there was Tadeusz Fiszbach, the secretary of the Regional Committee of Gdansk, who didn't exactly help us carry out a strike in 1980, but didn't stand in our way either. We didn't really understand ourselves back then what was going on within the party elite. But things had started to budge, somehow. During a Round Table meeting[22] one time I met Aleksandr Kwasniewski, whom I'd considered abhorrent until very recently. And suddenly it turned out that he was this very agreeable, genteel and intelligent man who understood everything perfectly! Crooks and thugs abounded among the Communists, of course, but there were other types too. Dariusz Rosati, for example – a very intelligent man. So we mustn't speak the language of the French Jacobins.[23] Everyone has to be given a chance.

Navalny Who first voiced the idea of a Round Table?

Michnik We were talking about a need to return to negotiations from the very first days of martial law. And we never renounced the path we'd always planned to take. Our strength was demonstrated at Popieluszko's funeral and during the strikes of 1988. We kept saying it wasn't a revolution we wanted, but reforms. So when the powers that be started giving us cautious signals, we put forward our conditions for dialogue. Yet, as Jaruzelski later confessed to me, the intelligence agencies were doing their usual disinformation job, and making us out to be radicals. So the process was a very slow one.

Navalny At a Round Table in 1989 you reached an agreement on two points: the legalisation of Solidarity and semi-free parliamentary elections.

Michnik And at the election we won 99 of 100 seats in the Senate and all 35% of contested seats in the Sejm.[24] Only Mao Zedong in China could boast that kind of result.

Navalny Was this a single-mandate election?

Michnik Yes, and almost all the candidates had their photo taken together with Wałęsa.

Navalny And the Communists allowed every candidate to stand? They didn't ban a single one?

Michnik Not one.

Navalny Putin's learned these lessons, and simply doesn't allow undesirable candidates anywhere near elections.

Michnik I'd hoped, of course, that the election campaign would prove a success, but I never thought it'd be as successful as *that*! The regime was crashing and burning! We were afraid they wouldn't accept defeat and dissolve the newly elected parliament. That's what the Egyptian military did in 2013. But the Communists didn't know what to do next.

Shortly after the election, but before the first meeting of the new parliament, a big reception was held; opposition MPs and senators as well as key Communist figures (Jaruzelski, Kiszczak, Rakowski and others) all attended. There, I was approached by Professor Janusz Rejkowsky, a party liberal who'd been brought into the Politburo in 1988. A very intelligent man, he was. And he said, "Mr Michnik, I know this hasn't yet been discussed, but what do you have to say on the subject of your future prime minister?" "I don't know," I said, "I'll have to ask my boss." So I went off to Wałęsa. Wałęsa said he was on board with it [that Solidarity would appoint its representative as prime minister], and that Geremek would be prime minister. Rejkowsky responded positively. And I realised only then – this wasn't some fantasy or absurdist scenario, it could actually materialise! I just hadn't grasped that they could possibly accept their absolute trouncing! But most of my colleagues took a very critical stance in this regard.

Navalny And why was that? What exactly did they want?

Michnik They didn't believe such a thing was possible. They wanted to remain in opposition, to scrutinise the regime and criticise it. And the first person to criticise me was Tadeusz Mazowiecki, who'd soon become the first non-Communist prime minister! There's our opportunity, I thought; we need to adopt the Napoleonic principle of *"On s'engage et puis on voit"* ["Commit yourself first, then see what happens"]. My idea was to instigate a new era and find a place in the new Poland for everyone save criminals, crooks and thieves. As for the latter, they're for the judiciary to handle, not politicians. Political intervention in the courts effectively means an end to the rule of law. That was my logic. At the time I was considering the Spanish transition to democracy, facilitated by consensus rather than violence. Later, I spoke with Prime Minister Gonzalez, who denied that the country had transitioned to democracy in any particular, idiosyncratically Spanish way. "Felipe," I told him, "you've done it now, there's no need for you to understand, but from where *we're* standing it's clear to see that a Spanish way does exist!" Even Lenin made use of the military expertise of White generals. We couldn't conduct ourselves worse than the Bolsheviks. Of course, there were plenty of radicals among our number who demanded reprisals against the old leadership.

Navalny A lot of people made these demands?

Michnik A great many. Most of them had kept a very low profile during the dictatorship.

Navalny Now that's very interesting. You served six years in jail under the "old regime" and forgave those who put you away. But for most ex-political prisoners this is psychologically very difficult! Looking at it from the outside, it could, I think, even be interpreted as a betrayal of your peers: "You've no right to forgive them on behalf of us all!" Such sentiments were voiced too, no doubt.

Michnik They sure were!

Navalny Could you please tell me about how you managed to strike a balance between radicals and moderates in the opposition ranks? For us in Russia this is an issue of considerable importance.

Michnik We were absolutely moderately-minded. We campaigned on a human-rights platform and made it clear from the outset that we'd be supporting workers' protests, and taking advantage of any opportunity to expand human rights. Yes, there were people among us who preferred the language of the Jacobins. But it's much easier to talk revolution than to actually make it happen. People with the least knowhow were the loudest mouthers-off.

Navalny But what if people tell you that dialogue is pointless, that it'll result in nothing more than futile half-measures, and that there's no getting around the need for radical renewal and revolution?

Michnik Revolution can only give birth to a new Bolshevism. What really is the fundamental difference between this radical and that radical? I like your strategy, it really does pose a threat to crooks and thieves. There is, I believe, only one intelligent riposte to the radicals – and that riposte takes the form of an actual concrete project, in the mould of the one we had in Poland. We had *samizdat*, we had our Flying University; we united people and educated them. The prospects for such endeavours in today's Russia are far more favourable than anything we enjoyed back then: Russia might be an authoritarian state, but it doesn't have anything like the censorship of the totalitarian Polish People's Republic. Putin is no Stalin; you can't even compare the two.

Navalny I've always said, over and over again, that Putin's main weapon isn't repression. We do have political prisoners, but only a handful. Putin's main weapon, rather, is his ability to bribe the population. Much like Gierek in the 1970s.

So when was Mazowiecki mooted as a potential prime minister?

Michnik Almost from the outset. Mazowiecki was very close to Lech Wałęsa. He was a so-called "official Catholic." For many years he served as the chief editor of the official Catholic monthly journal *Więź [Link]*, and had been elected deputy of the communist Sejm three times. Everybody knew him very well. Wałęsa put forward three candidates: Mazowiecki, Kuroń and Geremek.

Navalny Two radicals and one moderate.

Michnik Yes, and Mazowiecki was selected. It was only later that we realised what great changes had taken place. Soon I found myself in Moscow and, thanks to Marina Pavlova-Silvanskaya, I was received at the Communist Central Committee. I was the first Pole to ever enter the building on Staraya Square with a Solidarity badge pinned to my lapel. There I held talks with Alexander Tsipko, assistant to Central Committee secretary Alexander Yakovlev, the leading party liberal. I asked, "Do you think any government of Poland would be able to find a common language with the Soviet government?" "Yes," he replied, "as long as it's not opposed to the Soviet Union." But how could we be against the USSR? *Perestroika* and freedom had come our way from Moscow.

Navalny It's remarkable how intelligently the regime conducted itself in conceding defeat. And these are the same people who declared martial law in '81.

Michnik Back then I was an opponent of Jaruzelski. He was a hostage to his own biography, I think – which is exactly why he declared martial law.

Jaruzelski once told me, "I realised two things during the war. Firstly, that the Russian people can't be equated with the chekists[25] who arrested my father. They're my fellow combat veterans too. Secondly, I understood that Poland could exist on the map of Europe only as a pro-Soviet country." That was the difference between him and the Polish communists: while they believed Poland should be Soviet, he insisted that it should be *pro*-Soviet. He was never a bona fide communist. The *apparat* [party apparatus] was struggling against the dismantling of the Soviet system, and Jaruzelski represented the only guarantee for the hammer-and-sickle brigade that everything would end peacefully. Without him, the democratic transformation in Poland would have inevitably turned violent. "Doesn't matter whether Jaruzelski was a communist or an anti-communist," I was told by one Czech politician. "He was a Polish general, and we didn't have anyone like him." Later, Jaruzelski and I got to know each other really well; we went round to each other's houses. Many of my colleagues didn't get how I could maintain ties with someone of that ilk. But I understood the debt we owed him. I was no optimist twenty-five years ago and I was afraid the situation could've developed differently.

Incidentally, nothing would ever have happened without Gorbachev either.

Navalny Perceptions of Gorbachev in Russia differ markedly from the way he's perceived abroad. You've probably seen *The Lives of Others*, the famous German film depicting the activities of the Stasi[26] in East Germany. Near the end of the film one of the antagonists says their power's going to last for decades. And there's a close-up of a front page announcing Gorbachev's election as the new General Secretary. After listening to you now, I can answer the question everyone's been asking for the last twenty-five years: "Why was the West so fond of Gorbachev? He was, after all, hated in Russia!" We really did hate Gorbachev and we loved Yeltsin. Gorbachev was criticised for his silence and his indecision ...

Michnik But he opened the door!

Navalny From Russia it all looked different – like he'd obliterated everything. We saw the sappers' shovels they used to smash people over the heads, in Georgia and Lithuania.[27]

Michnik That wasn't his doing. Mikhail Sergeyevich is no liberal. He was part of the last generation of real Bolsheviks. But what happened in the Soviet Union demonstrated that top-down reforms are indeed possible. Gorbachev ushered in great change in Russia.

Navalny Gorbachev proclaimed *glasnost*[28] only when public pressure on the party became expedient for him due to the fact that the party apparatus was openly sabotaging his economic reforms. *Perestroika* in its familiar form was a movement initiated at the top with a view to enlist the support of society.

Michnik I agree. In this sense I believe change from above is indeed possible, but only provided societal pressure is at work too. We mustn't ever rule out this type of scenario. Power may be taken by people willing to allow far-reaching reforms for the sake of their own interest.

4

Lustration

Navalny In Russian opposition circles it is very widely believed that Yeltsin's main mistake was his failure to implement lustration. I know that lustration is something you're against. Yet in an old interview of yours you said that, in principle, you don't exclude the possibility of banning certain people from holding public office. Have you since changed your opinion?

Michnik I'm still opposed to lustration. The type of lustration we saw implemented in Czechoslovakia and Poland in the 1990s is tantamount to a moral crime, as well as representing an unquestionable error on the part of our democracy.[29] Transferring judicial powers to special institutions that base their activities on intelligence agency archives – well, that's pure Orwell. It's imperative these things remain within the framework of regular judicial proceedings. If you've credible evidence that a certain official or police officer or intelligence services agent has been breaking the law, you should apply to the prosecutor's office and initiate a regular trial. Have you read my interview with Václav Havel? He spoke out against unruly lustration practices too.

Navalny Let's pick a concrete example. Should the judge who jailed my brother by order of the Kremlin be lustrated?

Michnik. No. You'd need to establish a commission of lawyers and prepare a report into precisely what unlawful rulings the judge had made under Putin. You'd do this to demonstrate the obvious to everyone, to make everything clear and comprehensible. But that wouldn't be lustration, would it?

Navalny That'd be a fair administration of justice.

Michnik If, say, the fact of a particular crime is confirmed only by denunciations unearthed in security services archives, that crime cannot *a priori* be considered proven. The same goes for restricting people's rights simply as a result of their having collaborated with this or that organisation. You have to understand how security services files were compiled. Let's say some Mr X gets summoned into the agency and is asked, "What do you know about Japanese espionage?" "If I knew anything about it," he replies, "I would be the first to come and tell you." And a note is made in Mr X's file that he willingly expressed a desire to collaborate with the security services. Total trust in the archives of such bodies is tantamount to a logical error: under the "old regime" everybody was a liar and only the KGB (and its other incarnations) told the absolute truth!

Navalny You were a member of the parliamentary commission that examined the archives of the Polish Ministry of the Interior in 1990, weren't you?[30]

Michnik That's right. There were four historians on the commission. We didn't have access to everything. They only showed us documents that weren't relevant to the current state of affairs. But I did get a look at a few odds and ends, and it was a total nightmare! For example, there was a photo of a Japanese businessman in a hotel with a prostitute ... And then I realised that all this would have needed to be kept classified for the following fifty years – so the information would only see the light of day long after the demise of anyone involved. But on one condition: if a person is seeking a senior public post, the prime minister must have access to that person's entire file and bear responsibility for his nomination.

Navalny So it's not worth opening and publishing the secret files of persons seeking public office?

Michnik That's a very interesting question. Personally I'd say yes, it is worth it. But there's one caveat, and that concerns intimate archives. You know yourself how much dirt is poured on politicians who are in the public spotlight. It's one thing for the media to share information sourced through their own efforts, and it's quite another for them to make reference to the archive of a government agency. That'd be a very bad thing to do because all that information's been amassed in violation of the law. Government agencies have no right to keep tabs on my private life. I don't think information of that kind ought to be made public.

Navalny Yes, that's an important issue. I've the same point of view. Their secret files are indeed the product of unlawful activities. I've got FSB men on my tail, recording every second of my life – and afterward they'll be showing everyone what they've dug up. I think you'd need to establish a special commission consisting of highly esteemed individuals who'd be subject to secrecy requirements. They'd have the opportunity to scrutinise all the available material and make public only what's relevant, say, to elections – anything to do with people's private lives, their families or children, would be off limits.

Michnik And this commission would need its own historians, sociologists and so forth: you need to be clued up on various aspects of the material you're reading. There's the *content* of the source, but then there's also the *criticism* of the source, both internal and external. You need to understand exactly who wrote the denunciation and why, and to what extent that denunciation is accurate.

Navalny One of the strongest arguments in favour of lustration is that it satisfies an objectively existing public demand for justice.

Michnik Lustration isn't justice; it's revenge.

Navalny I think there's a certain terminological confusion here. In Russia the term *lustration* is very frequently understood to mean a procedure that can easily be carried out within the framework of a normal, fair trial. My position on this issue is therefore that everybody must be given a jury trial. More often than not, there's no need to resort to special laws to convict Putin's officials because they routinely violate even those laws that they themselves write and adopt.

Michnik I agree. It's always the courts, and not politicians, that must make the decision.

Navalny In the context of contemporary Russia, the lustration issue raises two important questions. The first concerns its purpose, which, for me, is to satisfy the demand for justice. It's not a question here of dealing with all security services agents in a space that's beyond the bounds of ordinary jurisdiction, for example. Security services agents (whether of the secret or regular varieties) are not in themselves targets of social aggression. We're talking about people who have committed crimes and must be fairly punished through the courts. And this process must be formalised because I don't think you can draw a definitive line under the past in its absence. Otherwise thousands of people will feel betrayed. Secondly, I agree that if you allowed me *personally* to carry out lustration, I could get carried away and add people I simply happened not to like onto my lustration list. We should therefore create a transparent procedure for the collection, and subsequent transfer to courts of regular jurisdiction, of case materials concerning people who oversaw political repression and violated even Putin's laws. I'm convinced that it's for the courts to determine whether or not they should have the opportunity to hold high-level political office in future.

Michnik Yes, and for the courts alone. But from the Polish point of view this wouldn't constitute lustration – it'd be an ordinary judicial procedure.

Navalny It's important for me to scout out some common ground between our positions. I mean, you don't endorse the idea of simply forgetting and forgiving those who only yesterday were putting us behind bars while proclaiming, *à la* Ghandi, that we've forgiven everyone for everything? I can forgive my own persecutors, but I've no moral right to forgive those who persecuted others. Lots of people are now behind bars as a result of their support for me, and I can't very well tell them, "Sorry, but I've forgiven your persecutors."

Michnik I do agree, of course. But I have to reiterate – these things must be determined through the courts alone.

Navalny Yes, and we have to understand that many of these are trials we're going to lose. It's something we need to be prepared for and accept. But I believe we should go for it anyway.

There's another particular aspect to future Russian lustration (let's stick to that term): the question of unlawful enrichment. In the rest of post-1989 Eastern Europe, this wasn't a problem on any serious scale. We know the *nomenklatura* [ruling class] had a better standard of living than rank-and-file citizens, but they never enjoyed the phenomenal riches of contemporary Russian officialdom. It's imperative that the UN Convention against Corruption[31] and the principle of retroactivity are both fully applied in cases involving these people, that the statute of limitations is repealed, etc.

Michnik I agree. But once again, this needs to be done through the courts.

Navalny Yes. The most important thing is to respect judicial procedure.

Michnik This really is an important issue for Russia. There were no multibillionaire officials in socialist Poland.

Navalny And in the USSR this wasn't a problem of massive proportions either. Now, I think, this type of lustration (though it's not lustration *per se*) would be supported by everybody. There may be convinced Stalinists in Russia, but there's no one in the country who approves of officials living like kings.

Michnik And yet I'd like to issue one more warning: whatever we mean by the term, lustration is a very delicate and complex matter. You need to be extremely cautious, steering well clear of radical dissident manoeuvres while not allowing yourself to be swayed by the logic of "cleansing." Plus, you have to handle any documentation from ex-state security services that may come into your possession, very carefully indeed. Who've they been collecting incriminating evidence against in recent years? Against a Petrov, an Ivanov, a Sidorov? No, of course not. Against Navalny. And who could fall victim to unruly lustration? In Poland, they tried to expose Lech Wałęsa as a secret agent of the Security Service![32] Over in Russia, you'll get radicals claiming that "Navalny is a Kremlin project" – either on account of their own stupidity or just to line their pockets.

Navalny Many people do say that.

Michnik I'm afraid of this Zeitgeist. Back in our day we drew a definitive line under the past and proposed the slogan "Amnesty Yes, Amnesia No!"[33] We can and should forgive, but we mustn't forget. There are people who were supporters of Putin before migrating into the ranks of the opposition ...

Navalny For instance, Mikhail Kasyanov was prime minister during Putin's first term, and now I'm setting up a democratic coalition with him.

Michnik That's an excellent example. Intelligence agencies spent twenty-five years looking for dirt on me. And they never found any. And not because I'm a saint but because, from their point of view, I was incorrigible. To them I was already dead and useless. I asked our Interior Minister Krzysztof Kozlowski whether they had anything on me. "Don't worry," he said, "just girls, and all pretty ones at that."

5

Gorbachev, Yeltsin, and Putin

Navalny I have to admit, over the past few years I've re-evaluated the events of the late 80s and early 90s. Back then I was a massive fan of Yeltsin's, but Gorbachev seems a far more appealing figure to me now. I understand what scenarios he could've put into effect – anything from bloodshed to stratospheric personal enrichment. He could've done everything Putin's doing now but didn't. He was detested by the whole country then, communists and liberals alike.

Michnik I can't forget that nothing whatsoever would have happened without Gorbachev. And I won't forget that it was *Yeltsin* who destroyed the ideology of Marxism-Leninism. Wałęsa and Yeltsin are similar figures, in my opinion. Back then Yeltsin embodied Russian-ness, he knew how to communicate with the people. And he was a genuine freedom-loving liberal. Wałęsa, too, was a man of the people with a knack for finding a common language with them. Both men headed democratic movements.

Poland was no Czechoslovakia, where the writer Václav Havel stood a chance of becoming president. They had Tomáš Masaryk; and they were ready to accept an intellectual president. It could be that in countries that lack a rich democratic tradition only men like Yeltsin and Wałęsa stand any chance of success. Poles and Russians love freedom. But neither Poles nor Russians understand that democracy is freedom within the framework of a rule-of-law state. And one keeps having to find the words to explain this to people.

Navalny What makes Wałęsa radically different from Yeltsin, though, is that while Wałęsa was the new man on the block, Yeltsin was a descendant of the old elite, who then turned against it – and won. The radical renewal of the elite we witnessed in Poland never happened in Russia.

Michnik You're right. But Yeltsin was a Sverdlovsk *apparatchik* [party bureaucrat], and from the Moscow *nomenklatura*'s point of view he *did* represent a newcomer. And he began behaving like one when he got to Moscow. Today, of course, his actions seem like those of a typical *apparatchik*, but in the context of Grishin-era Moscow, he was very much the new kid on the block. Then he was removed from his Politburo position, but no self-criticism was forthcoming from him. And he began to recall Pugachev[34] more than he did Brezhnev.[35]

Navalny There *were* certain instances of self-criticism on his part. But he really did have phenomenal political nous. Just like Wałęsa, he must've sensed instinctively what needed to be done and when.

Michnik No one ever imagined then that some "man on the street" could ever take power. Wałęsa was the leader of the strike in Gdansk, which is exactly what he is best remembered for. Of course, there's a difference between the Sverdlovsk Regional Committee and the Gdansk Shipyard. But Poland and Russia were both in need of charismatic leaders. I think the misfortune began when the Democrats lost the parliamentary elections to Zhirinovsky and Zyuganov in 1993. That was a psychological coup. Yeltsin couldn't guarantee the protection of his reformers, Gaidar[36] and Chubais.[37] Wałęsa, who had Solidarity's backing, was able to protect Balcerowicz.

Navalny That's not quite right. Chubais and Gaidar had Yeltsin's backing, and Yeltsin's significance for Russia was comparable to that of Solidarity for Poland.

Michnik But at some point he said, "Right, that's it, finito," and put them out to grass. People were saying then that there was no one in Russia worse than Chubais, that he was Russia's enemy no. 1. There's no more Bolsheviks or fascists, but there's Chubais, a more than ample replacement for them all.

Navalny As an erstwhile devotee of Yeltsin and Chubais I can say that Chubais arouses more negative emotions in me now than Putin does. It's to none other than Chubais, I believe, that we owe the existence of Putinism. He and others like him have perverted the meaning of the words "liberalism" and "democracy." It's because of them that these words are now being used to stigmatise democratic opposition. And this "liberal democrat" is now running a state-owned corporation while explaining to me that Putin and state ownership are good things.

Michnik And does Chubais support Putin?

Navalny Of course! After the murder of Boris Nemtsov, who only recently had been his closest ally, Chubais said that both sides – regime and opposition alike – needed to stop. And *he* – of all people – is telling me this!

During the 2007 Duma elections, Chubais said that the

nationalist Dmitry Rogozin was Russia's biggest enemy – and now he's working for the government in which Rogozin's serving as deputy prime minister. Ukraine, Crimea – it's all become the norm for him. It was absolutely criminal of Yeltsin to palm off Komsomols[38] and party activists on us in the guise of "liberals."

Michnik Tell me, Alexei, where are you going to find other liberals in Russia? Our former Prime Minister Donald[39] was a prominent liberal oppositionist during the dictatorship, and later he founded the Liberal Democratic Congress party. But he forgot the word "liberalism" once he became prime minister. I think it's a question of political expediency. I understand where you're coming from. But if the democratic opposition comes to power in Russia, you'll realise that you're in a minority in the country and that you need to seek out allies. And your allies, I think, will be people like Chubais and Gaidar.

Navalny Gaidar and Chubais are completely different people. Gaidar's a liberal and Chubais isn't. He's just a hypocrite.

Michnik But a talented one at that!

Navalny There's a lot of talented people around. I think you need to follow Václav Havel's lead – prioritise morality and ethics and bring *honest* people into your team, rather than those who are just going to flout all their own principles like Chubais, who was a Komsomol member in Soviet times, then became a Yeltsinite democrat, and is a Putinist today.

Michnik Yes, but he was one of the most talented individuals in that contingent. In the given circumstances it'd be impossible to create a viable coalition without someone of his ilk in its ranks.

Navalny The question is whether to gamble on people like that. We had a human rights movement during *perestroika*, but then all the activists and dissidents were completely marginalised. I have to admit that I too sometimes find it hard to communicate with them – they've the air of neighbourhood crazies. But it's precisely because they've this crazy air about them that they got forced out by the *apparatchiks*. It seemed the right thing to do back then. I myself once believed that we were in need of unscrupulous yet – on the face of it – highly effective individuals like Chubais. It was a mistake to believe that. Perhaps you really can't get by without people like that on your team, but under no circumstances should you be staking anything on them. Yeltsin took a chance on people who plundered everything, before selling us all out to Putin in return for money and security for his family.

Michnik It's not that he "sold you out," exactly. I think he just realised he'd lost. When Putin became prime minister and then president, none of my Russian colleagues, even those working in the Kremlin, could have imagined how everything would turn out. Putin hadn't evinced any leadership qualities. He was a KGB lieutenant colonel; these people have a completely different mindset, different habits of conscience.

Navalny That's a very interesting issue. You mentioned that Wojciech Jaruzelski was heir to the military traditions of the Second Polish Republic – a real Polish general with a strong understanding of honour and duty. Two officers, but what an absolute chasm between them! Putin, too, presents himself as the country's saviour. He claims that the country was on the verge of collapse when he came to power, and that he prevented it from ruin.

Michnik The first four years he was in power, I thought all this wasn't complete bull and that there really was something in that claim. But I didn't fully see what was behind the explosions.[40] Many argued it was the work of the security agencies – an echo of the war with the oligarchs. Berezovsky and Gusinsky aren't exactly my cup of tea, and perhaps waging battle against them really was a necessity. But I didn't understand what exactly transformed Putin to such an extent?

Navalny I think the first changes in his character occurred in the wake of the Kursk tragedy.[41] That's when he saw the power of public opinion, and it frightened him. Everything seems to be going okay, it's all under control, but then some random accident happens, there's some black swan event, and suddenly it's out of your hands. People don't like you anymore and ask questions you struggle to answer. Putin realised that public opinion is a terrible force. And immediately after that he began tightening the screws on the media. 2003 saw the final destruction of NTV.[42] Perhaps Putin got scared by the political ambitions of Khodorkovsky, the most powerful of the oligarchs. Everything changed definitively in 2004 after the first Maidan.[43] I was already involved in politics at the time – I was a member of Yabloko. I remember us going down to the Ukrainian embassy in Moscow and giving the Ukrainians our support. After that year's Maidan, political freedoms in Russia began evaporating by the day. The Kremlin was scared witless – Ukraine's right on our doorstep. Everything seemed to be under control, only to collapse in a matter of days.

Michnik I agree. Putin is terribly afraid of the power of public opinion. I was watching Russian television during the first days of the [second] Maidan. It was constantly being emphasised that an analogous situation would be impossible in Russia because all the necessary measures would immediately be taken to prevent it. Putin's worst nightmare is a Maidan on Red Square. Someone told me about Putin's reaction upon seeing a broadcast of Mubarak in the dock: he had an absolute fit; he just refused to believe such a thing was even *possible*. And he had the same reaction after the killing of Gaddafi. He's haunted by a very deep-seated fear of a "meaningless and merciless Russian rebellion."[44]

And really, if you look at twentieth-century Russian history, this is the eternal subject of reflection by the Russian intelligentsia: think back to *Vekhi* [*Landmarks*] and *From the Depths*.[45] It's from Russia, and not from the West, that the idea of non-violent struggle made its way over to us in Poland.

Navalny This is a very interesting point as well, because, in a sense, Putin has taken this on board. He's always saying, "Guys, you realise what alternative we have, right? Take me out of the picture and we have a 'meaningless and merciless Russian revolt' on our hands! Navalny will turn up and there'll be rivers of blood!" It's a sort of bloody mythologem, I think. Why must a "Russian revolt" be the alternative to Putin's dictatorship? This mythologem is deliberately being imposed on public consciousness, and even *you* say there's something in it. I'm convinced any "Russian revolt" is more likely to be catalysed by hypocritical stability, by regime-stoked social acrimony, and by the systematic suppression of any real opposition.

Michnik I agree. But it's also clear to me that the democratic opposition must adopt a kind of principle of nonviolence and stress repeatedly that it doesn't want a revolution. I'm not saying Putin's departure *will* bring about a terrible Russian revolt. I'm saying this is one of the possible scenarios. The inevitable collapse of the current regime will open the door not only to the democratic opposition, but also to people like Strelkov and Zakharchenko – people who'll hang you all as liberals and cosmopolites. A potential scenario resembles what happened in Iran, where conservatives spoke the language of revolution. In Russia, Alexander Dugin – to cite one example – is a proponent of this kind of conservative-revolutionary project. And he now has very close links to the Kremlin. Similar inclinations have been noted in the work of Aleksandr Solzhenitsyn, whom I respect very much. What do you think of the National Bolsheviks,[46] for example?

Navalny They're an unconventional party, and one which doesn't actually exist. They're better described as Eduard Limonov's art project. Despite the fact that they've practically managed to secure legal status for themselves on account of the events in Ukraine, they stand no chance of electoral success. Limonov's idea is to oppose the liberal mainstream: if all the liberals like Yeltsin, Limonov doesn't; if the liberals don't like Putin, Limonov loves him.

Michnik And he's supporting Putin now?

Navalny In respect of Ukraine and Crimea, absolutely. Limonov's now a columnist for the semi-official newspaper *Izvestia*. As far as the presidential administration is concerned, Limonov is an acceptable opposition figure, akin to Zyuganov and Zhirinovsky. But as for Navalny, Kasyanov and others, they're *un*acceptable oppositionists – the "fifth column" – and their destruction is a desirable objective. Limonov himself has now entered the political mainstream – he makes television appearances and enjoys column inches. So his party poses no real threat to anyone.

How about the opposition landscape in Poland? Who represents an alternative to the ruling Civic Platform?

Michnik Poland has its own problems. President Bronislaw Komorowski's a conservative Catholic, but he's a highly responsible individual and he has my support because his opponents – the right-wing conservative opposition, Kaczyńskis' Law and Justice party[47] – are Putinists in essence and Zhirinovskyites in terms of their rhetoric. Five years ago I presented a report on Poland in Russia in which I called Jaroslaw Kaczyński, Warsaw's answer to Putin. I see only one main difference: while Kaczyński is a misfortune for Poland, Putin is a misfortune for the entire world. In terms of his psychology, Kaczyński's a dyed-in-the-wool Polish Putinist. His idea of a state without a democratic opposition is absolutely Putinist in character.

There's a handful of far-right parties in Poland – an example is Janusz Korwin-Mikke's party,[48] which has representation in the European Parliament. There are also radical unofficial organisations – the anti-systemic opposition. They're not particularly dangerous on their own, but they could potentially join forces with Kaczyński to form an anti-democratic coalition, though I'm sure there'd be in-fighting among them too. That's their psychology. But they could destroy the democratic order, destabilise the country, bring everything down to the level of farce. I'll do everything I can to ensure their defeat. But if they do succeed, Poland could face a Hungarian or a Russian scenario, by which I mean the Orbánisation[49] or Putinisation of the country. Russia has everything: political parties, a press, a parliament. But it's all a sham, one big "Potemkin village." The same can't quite be said of Hungary just yet, but they're heading in the same direction. It's amazing how [Hungarian Prime Minister] Viktor Orbán has fallen in love with Putin! That unbelievable thief [former Italian prime minister] Berlusconi was just as hot for him before.

Navalny They've been united by corruption. An equivocation has taken place in Russia. All the failures of the 1990s – and especially those that occurred in the transition phase – have been blamed on the "liberals" who were allegedly in power at the time. And now, whenever the issue of the regime's changeability is broached, they start telling their horror-stories about the "wild 1990s" and the liberals' plundering of the country, thereby proving the necessity of keeping assets under state control and extending their time in power, which they use for one purpose only – to commit thievery on a colossal scale.

The new Poland and the new Russia both began with a period of shock therapy.[50] How did Poland come through this experience, and how has a social consensus materialised regarding these radical transformations?

Michnik A good economic school emerged in Poland even before the reforms. Young economists were already doing research, writing articles and organising seminars at a time when no one took them seriously. People later said that to all intents and purposes it was Jeffrey Sachs rather than Leszek Balcerowicz who was really responsible for the reforms. But that's nonsense. Sachs did advise Balcerowicz, but the idea of implementing the reforms was Leszek's, and he bore full responsibility for it. The central argument in favour of radical reforms was to do with the catastrophic economic situation in Poland.

Navalny I've read what Poland's per capita GDP (PPP) was in 1990: just three quarters of Russia's.[51]

Michnik Shock therapy brought positive results! But then a fierce campaign was unleashed against Balcerowicz. Having won the 1990 presidential election, Wałęsa kept him on as finance minister and appointed the liberal Jan Bielecki prime minister. Those ex-Communists that returned to power also sharply criticised Balcerowicz's policies, but not the general direction of the reforms. President Kwaśniewski announced a policy of careful continuity, stipulating that it was indeed necessary to keep moving in the same direction, but not at such a rapid pace. It's in this sense, perhaps, that we can speak of some kind of consensus, but by no means a total one! I was a proponent of Balcerowicz's shock therapy, and our newspaper endorsed his policies.

Now I realise the mistake inherent in our handling of the transition: we failed to find a common language with the people, and couldn't explain to society why things were so difficult then. [Minister of Labour and Social Policy] Jacek Kuroń was an exception. He'd make TV appearances every Tuesday, explaining what had happened, what problems we'd now be facing, and what we needed to do. People wanted to know what was going on, and they trusted him.

Navalny Gaidar also failed to achieve this. But is it even possible in a society without censorship? Every time Balcerowicz or Gaidar set out to explain the essence of a government policy, their opponents were invited by the media to criticise these decisions live on air. In a free society, can expository state propaganda be disseminated in this way?

Michnik Things were even more problematic in Poland – in addition to the media, the strong, influential Solidarity was another crucial player, and the way Solidarity communicated with Balcerowicz was similar to the way the Communist party had talked to the government before. Balcerowicz didn't like trade unions and believed that their absence played what was perhaps a key role in the economic success of south-east Asian countries. In my opinion, however, you can and must find the right words. Everybody will be against you, of course, and you'll need to tell people honestly that you need, say, four more years, to make the time horizon clear. And you mustn't forget about the most vulnerable citizens, either. In Poland, that meant miners and the elderly.

Navalny Ditto in Russia.

Michnik That's exactly the problem. The Communists returned to power on a wave of radical discontent with reforms. They kept reminding the public of the fact that there'd been no unemployment during the socialist era. I'm still not entirely clear as to what would've become of Russia had Yeltsin lost the presidential election to Zyuganov in 1996?

Navalny That's one of the key questions we're currently thinking about. In those days, I was an ardent Yeltsinite and applauded when Yeltsin stormed the Supreme Soviet building in 1993[52] and rigged the elections of '96.[53] Now I'm one of the few people to have publicly expressed regret at having given him my support. Thinking about it all philosophically, I regard my prosecution, my brother's imprisonment and the persecution of the opposition as a kind of karma for the fact that I once backed all these measures. Perhaps we needed to have gone through the same thing as Eastern Europe did – the return to power of the Communists in one form or another. Then the pendulum swung once again, and they gave way to others. There's nothing threatening about alternations of power. I think it wasn't the Communists we vanquished in 1996, it was the elections themselves. It was then that the Kremlin ordered the governors to falsify the election results in favour of Yeltsin. The governors liked the sound of this, and later they'd be rigging results not only in favour of the Kremlin but in their own as well. Having taken control of the electoral mechanisms, they were able to extend their time in power by decades. But back in 1996, it seemed we had to do everything we possibly could to ensure a Yeltsin victory. And that's when we lost the opportunity for an Eastern European-style transition. The upshot of it all was this curious stretch of countries whose leaders all enjoy incredibly high ratings and voter support: Kazakhstan, Uzbekistan, Tajikistan and Russia. It's a great tragedy for us all, though it's difficult for many people to admit that we were fundamentally wrong back then. In 1993 and 1996 we were told that, were it not for Yeltsin, the red-browns [communists-fascists] would be taking power, waging repression against the people and starting wars aimed at the restoration of the Soviet empire. And what do we have on our hands now? We didn't let the red-browns storm parliament and destroy the elections, but the imperial wars began anyway. I therefore think it's crucial for the Russian opposition to re-evaluate the events of 1993 and 1996. Yeltsin's opponents had a repulsive air about them back then, no doubt about that. And when I saw them on TV, I agreed they should be shot – that Yeltsin must win at any price. But now it seems to me that it would've been no catastrophe for them to win in those elections, and that the Communists would inevitably have been swept from power next time around.

Michnik Do you think the Zyuganovites would have gone down the constitutional road?

Navalny They kept within constitutional limits.

Michnik Up to a certain juncture Hitler did too!

Navalny We've got what we've got. Yeltsin catalysed the liquidation of fair and transparent elections, and established a system of electoral fraud. And Yeltsin enabled the coming to power of Putin, who has employed that self-same system to build up an authoritarian regime. The fundamental point is that politicians shouldn't be allowed to rig elections – even for the sake of battling against the "bad guy" Zyuganov. Society accepted these falsifications back then. It was then that the schoolteachers who today are responsible for overseeing the voting procedures at polling stations became acquainted with the practice for the first time. The mechanisms that were honed then are still in force today. That was our big mistake. We undermined public confidence in the institution of elections. Incidentally, Putin's regime is exploiting this issue to its own advantage. The current chairman of the Constitutional Court – Valery Zorkin, who's endorsed absolutely every one of Putin's clearly unconstitutional and repressive laws – recently penned a long article[54] in which he virtually accused the liberal community, the people who'd supported the storming of the White

House in 1993, of bringing about the lawlessness that's rife today. According to this logic, I – who was a student back then – have been prosecuted and barred from elections because of Yeltsin's storming of parliament. Meanwhile, the democratic opposition is being vilified for the same reason – Yeltsin, after all, styled himself a "democrat" and a "liberal." We're going to be scaling this obstacle for a very long time yet. An important moral challenge facing the opposition is that of calling things by their proper name, and condemning what happened in 1993 and 1996.

Michnik Alexei, what you're saying seems spot on to me, and very important too. With this type of thinking, we've real prospects for the future.

Navalny I'm very glad our views coincide as far as the fundamentals are concerned.

6

Corruption as an Institution

Michnik I think you're right in calling the current political elite a "party of crooks and thieves." But there's one problematic aspect to this slogan: figures of the Hitler or Lukashenko breed have been prone to similar kinds of rhetoric.

Navalny And back in the day, Yeltsin used it too. It's true, many dictators and authoritarian leaders began their political career as fighters against corruption and the privileges of those in power. I realise that.

Michnik But in Yeltsin's case – unlike Lukashenko's – these slogans were integrated into the context of a democratic movement. Therefore it's very important that both sides of the coin feature in your political programme: we're against corruption because we stand for democracy and the rule of law. Even Prokhanov can scream "Down with the thieves!"

Navalny I completely agree! This is a very important question for me. I don't often express my views on the subject because it seems self-evident to me – there's only one effective way of vanquishing corruption, and that's to build a democracy. For me, there'd be no tangible difference as such between anti-corruption endeavours and political activities.

Michnik That's absolutely true.

Navalny I'm convinced that corruption can be eradicated only if four conditions are fulfilled: the ruling regime must be easily replaceable, elections fair and transparent, the judiciary independent, and the media free. Corruption can't be defeated by purely technical or operative-investigative means, only democratic ones. The idea I'm trying to get across to people is that the problem of corruption isn't limited to budget losses. It's not purely a question of mathematics. The problem isn't that someone's stolen a load of money and built themselves a palace, but rather that corruption leads to the collapse of state institutions. Corrupt officials don't perform their direct duties properly – they're completely absorbed by their own thievery. Their value systems, goal-setting initiatives and motivations become totally warped. As a result, the state that was created to provide for the diverse needs of society turns into something that does the opposite: an instrument of plunder. And until we build a proper democratic state we won't solve the problem of corruption.

Michnik I completely agree.

Navalny But this isn't that easy to explain. It's much easier to adopt a populist stance: "Crooks will be shot." Today we see that Putin's constantly flirting with the prospect of restoring the death penalty. But what's the point of executing someone for corruption? After all, it's not the existence of the punishment that matters, but the *inevitability* of said punishment! In theory you can already get 10 or 20 years for corruption today, but that's not putting the frighteners on anyone.

Michnik Meting out death sentences for corruption is the Chinese way of doing things.

Navalny And yet China's a highly corrupt country. Because you can't defeat corruption without a free media that'll ensure societal pressure. And then the mechanism of regime change through elections should kick in. Nowadays people often talk about the experience of Singapore, which has defeated corruption while maintaining an authoritarian regime ...

Michnik But Singapore's effectively a city, not a country!

Navalny Exactly! Its small scale, together with the requisite political will, allowed Lee Kuan Yew to defeat corruption without creating democratic institutions.[55] But larger states require fundamentally different solutions. And at this point I'd like to ask you a question: what do you consider of greatest importance in the construction of a new democratic state? Which institutions need to be developed first?

Michnik Firstly, you need to carry out judicial reform. And here, of course, you'd need a specific type of lustration. You'd definitely have to get rid of the judges and prosecutors who played a role in the criminal practices of the Putin regime. But this'd be a job for an internal commission. It's not something that could be done in one day – the process is a very complicated one, and you'd need to do it step by step. In Poland this wasn't implemented to the fullest degree. Not all judges in the communist era were mere puppets controlled by the regime. There were some, though. The judge who sentenced me in Gdansk subsequently found himself in the dock. But I refused to testify against him, arguing I couldn't be objective with regard to a man who had sentenced me. There were plenty of other witnesses, anyway.

It's hugely important to ensure the non-interference of the state in the media. Putin's destruction of NTV signalled the fact that nothing good was in store for Russia. You'd also need a large-scale anti-corruption campaign extending to all spheres of life: industry, education, and so forth. I'm sure you're familiar with this issue and have the personnel to implement such a campaign. There'd also need to be new legislation regarding political parties to ensure they couldn't be destroyed so easily.

Navalny I think the basic difference between Russia and Poland during their respective periods of transformation has to do with the fact that we never went beyond an economic metamorphosis – there was no genuine transformation of a *political* kind. Granted, the Communist party was banned in the wake of the August coup, and a constitution proclaiming Russia a democratic state was adopted, but fraud was prevalent as early as the 1996 presidential elections; and there'd always been fraud at the regional level – even during the romantic *perestroika* period. The courts, just like the regional media, were very much under the thumb of the regime. This lack of fundamental change is precisely why the pendulum's swung back in the other direction.

I completely agree that the main issue is judicial reform. Societal existence entails endless conflict, and if there's no institution that resolves conflicts within the framework of the established notions of justice (the framework of the law, that is), then social crises are inevitable. There has to be some legal authority that can rule in my favour or Putin's. If I lose, I walk away from politics, and this should apply to everyone. The court system is the crucial thing – without a properly functioning judiciary even the best laws wouldn't be respected and no reforms (whether economic, political, etc.) would be possible.

Russia's got a specific media-related problem as well: in all post-socialist countries the media managed to rid itself of state influence while safeguarding its independence, while in Russia the media was bought up by the oligarchs. But then the government subjugated all the oligarchs and get hold of their media assets. I think specific temporary regulation would need to be introduced in Russia to prohibit large companies (and especially resource companies) such as Gazprom and Lukoil from owning media outlets. We all understand only too well why these people need the media – they use it as an instrument of political influence.

Michnik That's exactly right!

Navalny We went through all this in the 1990s. The media's a very specific kind of business – in fact, it's not even a business as such since it's too unequivocally oriented toward achieving the public good. And I believe there should be limits on oligarchic structures, just as there should be limits on the government. You want to go into gas or oil? Be my guest. But you can't go into oil *and* into the media at the same time. You'd need these restrictions in place for a certain period at least.

Michnik Ukraine's a classic example. The oligarchs there have their own media, their own businesses, and now their own army as well.

Navalny So we've got to be very clear on the subject: the media is too fragile and too important an institution to be owned by oil-and-gas tycoons.

Finally, we need to provide all politicians and political

parties with the opportunity to participate in elections. If a party isn't inciting violence, it should have the chance to take part in elections regardless of its ideology. If it has support, it's entitled to parliamentary representation. We have to learn to negotiate with everyone – and to do so without fraud, repression or violence.

7
The Russian Idea

Michnik I think you've correctly identified Russia's principal problem – it is indeed corruption, which a great many people are implicated in. Ukrainian students come to study in the Polish town of Rzeszow,[56] and their first year they'll be going to their exams with envelopes stuffed full of money. In their native Ivano-Frankivsk, passing exams is next to impossible without passing money to the right people. And I'm sure Ukrainian students aren't the only ones facing this problem.

Navalny It's a typical problem across post-Soviet space.

Michnik Perhaps these things don't happen in Moscow and St Petersburg now, but you need to keep a close eye on such goings-on. I was thinking about why you command such authority, Alexei. Unlike many Russian writers, you don't go telling the Russian people that they're nothing but filth. You recognise the dignity in others, and you leave it up to them whether to be honest people or not. We just need to tell the truth – there's no need to set the people against the Putinists and instigate a new 1937.[57]

Navalny The more actively the authorities deploy the language of ideology – an empire, "our own way," etc – the more stubbornly do we have to keep to simple ideas and principles: don't lie, don't steal … In the words of Václav

Havel, the truth represents the best weapon against a state founded on supreme lies.[58] I really like this idea of his, which he expressed in an interview with you, that the age of ideologies is drawing to a close and an era of ideas is dawning.[59]

Michnik The "our own way" ideology is of great importance for Putin, and this is highly dangerous for the country. Thinking about the future, the real threat to Russia isn't Europe or the US – it's radical Islamism, and China.

Navalny That's a very important thought, because for me the main point of divergence between "us" and "them" rests on the question of whether or not to opt for the European path of development. Putin is trying to foist this point of view on us, which holds that there's a certain European ideology, and that this ideology is wholly alien as far as Russia's concerned. I'm opposed to this. I don't understand what Putin's ideology of a "special Russian path" actually means.

Michnik He'd tell you that it's to do with being a sovereign democracy.[60]

Navalny Right then, let's break this "sovereign democracy" concept down. What does "sovereign democracy" mean?

Michnik It appears to mean being able to jail all your opponents without having to answer to Strasbourg or what have you.

Navalny That's exactly what I'm saying. There's no positive ideology there. It's just another mythologem that's being imposed on society. When we start asking what exactly this "special path" actually entails in practice, they've no answer to give us. And that's because all this "special path" entails is the possibility of tyrannising any given individual at any given time. We're trying to reincorporate this question into a non-ideological context, which is exactly where it belongs. If we take any Russian individual who speaks about a special path in the context of an opinion poll, we'll see that this individual has European preferences all across the board. China isn't going to be close to his heart. And it's important for us to explain that the issue isn't an ideological one: Russians coming back from Germany or Poland all say that everything's calm and stable there, and that they want to live the same way. Nobody speaks about China with the same admiration.

Michnik Nobody but the *apparatchiks*, that is.

Navalny I think they fantasise about living in a "Europe" themselves while consigning the rest of us to a "China."

Michnik They fantasise about the society they run being as placid as China's.

Navalny But the Chinese elites are looking westward – they want to have Western lifestyles themselves.

Michnik Absolutely right.

Navalny We can see how the "special path" ideology acquires an imperialist character. It was very interesting for me to hear you say that, "we in Poland never mentioned the Soviet Union because we were afraid." It made me think that if you were to say the same thing on Russian TV, the majority of Russians would go, "Well, now *that's* happiness for you! They were afraid of us! There was Michnik, sitting there in Poland, I didn't even know what he looked like, and yet he was afraid of me." And that's a terrible state of affairs, and one we need to struggle against.

Michnik It really is a very sad, very dangerous thing. Because at the end of the day it'll be a tragedy for Russia. I made an appearance on Polish TV recently, and I was asked – in reference to the strong support for Putin indicated by opinion polls – why it is that the Russians love dictatorship. I replied that those self-same surveys also indicate that the war with Ukraine is backed by an absolute minority of Russians.[61] I've always said that surveys are a very deceptive thing. It's nonsense that "the Russian soul loves an iron fist." That's just idiocy.

Navalny Even in practical politics it's clear that the reality isn't even remotely close. Just yesterday there was an election in the Moscow region. It was the usual story: fraud, punch-ups at polling stations, barred observers, and so forth.[62] Imperialist ideology and the "special path" don't guarantee support for regime candidates. Because everyone wants the city mayor to be electable. Of course, it's difficult to compare the situations of Russia and Poland – Russia's a former colonial power, and we have intense nostalgia for "the great Soviet empire," so "feared and respected" by all and sundry. Putin is now skilfully exploiting this nostalgia, and his ideology has no other meaning than that.

Michnik I completely agree. And ordinary Russians don't gain anything from this chimera.

Navalny I think one of the challenges facing me is to create a type of patriotism that could exist without the invasion of

Czechoslovakia, Poland or Ukraine by Russian tanks. There's plenty of stuff Russia needs to be developing within the country itself. It's abominable: you travel through the European part of the country and you pass through totally neglected swathes of land, overgrown with birches. We're the largest country in the world; we don't need to expand beyond our borders. We've much to be proud of beyond the violence we've wreaked in other countries. I was very pleased to come across enthusiastic pronouncements about Russian culture in your interviews!

Michnik I'm a real anti-Soviet Russophile!

Navalny If we're in need of any expansion at all, it is, I think, expansion of the cultural kind. Science and art is what we were practically the best in the world at! And it's science and art that can bring us the recognition and renown we so crave. And it needn't involve hatred or the impoverishment of the population.

This, I believe, is what our primary goal should be. And people are ready for it. Judging by serious sociological surveys, the majority of the population believes that it's *within* the country itself that great power status comes to be forged.[63] It's all about the competitiveness of the economy, public prosperity, our cultural level, and it's got nothing to do with intervention in other countries. The majority of Russians believe that a great country is one whose people live well. But instead, other ideas are being imposed on us.

Michnik A street in Warsaw was recently named in honour of Osip Mandelstam.[64] I was invited to the naming ceremony, where I read a poem of his:

Take me into the night where the Yenisei
 flows,
Where the pine tops touch the stars,
Because my blood isn't a wolf's blood,
And only an equal will kill me.[65]

And I said I was glad the Polish capital was playing host to the sounds of the Russian language, and glad, too, that the words being spoken were Mandelstam's and not Brezhnev's.

Navalny That's wonderful!

8

Nationalism

Michnik In Europe you're regarded as a nationalist. Could you clarify your position on this matter?

Navalny Many people regard me as a nationalist in Russia as well. These are mainly people who find it comforting to live in a world of ideological clichés. There are some topics that're considered virtually taboo in liberal circles – issues surrounding migration, for instance. I believe Russia should introduce a visa regime with Central Asian countries and keep tight control over labour migration.

Michnik Is there currently no visa regime?

Navalny There isn't, no. And my nationalism in this regard consists of nothing more than an advocacy of such a regime, which, among other things, would bolster migrants' rights in practice. Because if we filtered the stream of incomers through a visa regime, migrants would be forced to get work permits and take out medical insurance. And then they'd be able to count on legal and medical assistance if they needed it. The situation we have today is completely unmanageable. Let's say an illegal migrant gets his hand cut off on a construction site: what's he supposed to do? Just die in the gutter? No one's going to treat him. I believe Russia should look to the experience of civilised countries and make use of instruments such as visas and work quotas. That'd be a start.

Looking at the issue more broadly, my thinking is that we need to communicate with nationalists and conduct explanatory work among them. By no means all nationalists in Russia are driven by a clear-cut ideology. They just identify some general injustice or other, and respond to it by directing aggression against people of a different colour and/or eye-shape. I believe it's essential to explain to them that the problem of illegal migration is going to be solved not by violence against migrants but by other methods entirely – democratic methods such as the reinstatement of competitive elections, through which we can rid ourselves of the crooks who profit from illegal immigration.

I've devoted a great deal of energy to this issue. At one point, Russian nationalism even began to evolve into conservatism of an entirely European kind. Unfortunately, Putin destroyed all that, and mainstream Russian nationalism is once again leaning towards imperialism. I've been to a lot of nationalist meetings and participated in the Russian Marches, for which I've been castigated by many Russians and virtually branded a fascist, but, prior to 2014, none of these ever featured any slogans regarding Crimea or Ukraine. The question of Crimea wasn't on the nationalist agenda. What *did* receive serious discussion, for example, was the problem of defending Russians' rights in Uzbekistan and Chechnya.

Michnik And in the Baltics as well?

Navalny Predominantly from a linguistic perspective. Everyone realised that Russians in Estonia, for example, wouldn't want to return to the Russian fold, even if they were proclaiming their love for Putin. There was an absolute consensus in nationalist circles back then that Russia's main problem was the current state of the country: the degradation of the population, alcoholism, the declining birth rate, etc, and that these problems had to be solved by the implementation of various domestic measures, not by means of foreign policy. The birth rate in Russia is among the lowest in the world, and that's an issue that needs resolving. But for many liberal politicians the national agenda was of marginal importance. In the end, Putin put forward a fundamentally different project, an imperialist one, and co-opted these people. We lost contact with them. Between 2011 and 2013, the nationalists went with us to protest rallies and supported the idea of giving everyone the right to stand for election. They brandished slogans like "For Democracy!" and spoke out in favour of judicial reform and a free media. Yes, they've got a bizarre air about them, and the "back catalogue" of their pronouncements makes for scary listening. But I still believe we need to maintain a dialogue with them. Otherwise the regime can easily sway them over to the "let's take over the whole world" mode of thinking. External expansion, the split between Russia and America/Europe, and so forth – these have once again become the cornerstones of Russian nationalism.

Imperialist nationalism is the most toxic and dangerous of all the varieties of nationalism. It has to be combated. But we have to understand that there cannot be a vacuum. Everywhere you go there'll be a conservative, national-oriented segment of the population, and these people need to be provided with an alternative project – a civic nationalism predicated not on physiology or a sense of national superiority, but on universal civil rights and freedoms, and the potential to determine the fate of our country together. And this is a real possibility. I've invested a lot of effort into this and hope to be able to re-establish some kind of dialogue. So far, admittedly, I've accomplished nothing but damage to my own image. I'm branded a nationalist by liberals and a liberal by nationalists. And everyone has me down as a fifth columnist.

Michnik If only Poland had more nationalists like Navalny. I don't think the word "nationalist" has purely negative connotations. For me a nationalist is, first and foremost, someone who has respect for national honour. And in this regard I'm a nationalist as well.

Navalny In your articles and interviews, you always emphasise the double-edged nature of Polish nationalism: it can be a big plus on the one hand, but, on the other, it's a massive minus, and nationalism can be very dangerous.

Michnik There are many aspects to this issue. First, you need to understand the difference between nationalism and patriotism. Patriotism means that I love my country and my people, and I don't think that entering into conflict with other nations is going to do my own any good. So patriotism as I see it involves improving relations with my country's neighbours and with ethnic minorities inside the country. But there's another conception of the issue, too: [for the Catholic Church] Poland is the Catholic state of the Polish nation, and therefore a true citizen of Poland is a pure blooded, ethnically Polish Catholic.[66] If you're a Protestant rather than a Catholic, that's bad enough; and and if you're of Jewish, Ukrainian, Belarusian, Lithuanian or German descent, that's *really* bad. The debate about what constitutes Polish national identity isn't over. Our current Constitution refers to "We, the Polish nation – all citizens of the republic ..." This is the political conception of what constitutes a nation. But there are supporters aplenty of the ethno-religious interpretation.

Secondly, there's the issue of understanding and interpreting the history of your country. Some parallels with Russia can be drawn in this regard: many people in Poland are convinced that we intrinsically cannot be to blame – we've never done ill to anyone, we've only ever sacrificed ourselves. In 2001, Professor Jan Tomasz Gross published his book *Neighbours*, which investigates the massacre of the Jews of Jedwabne by the town's Polish inhabitants in July 1941.[67] This book spawned a stormy debate in Poland, with many declaring Gross a Polonophobe, and denying the veracity of the evidence cited in the book. I've said time and time again that we have to speak the truth about our own history. This serves to endow the nation with dignity and demonstrates that we're not afraid of the truth, and take it on board like adults. Not everyone in Poland is prepared to do this.

Thirdly, nationalism could provoke conflicts with neighbouring states and render the country insular and closed-off. Historically, Poland's relations with Russia, Ukraine, Lithuania and Germany have been anything but simple, and we have to be able to admit we've been wrong on some historical issues.

Nationalism in the communist era was extremely crude in nature, branding anyone open to outside influence as fifth columnists, rootless cosmopolitans, or traitors to the Motherland. And yet our national communists were lackeys of the Soviet Union, because they understood that Moscow was the guarantor of Poland's western border. They were ready to obey Moscow's orders, but they didn't want the country to be Sovietised. Ceaușescu represented their ideal. Then, in the era of Solidarity, anti-Soviet patriotism entered the scene. People didn't declare these sentiments openly, of course – we were afraid. But everyone was rooting for independence by then. We printed the truth about the Soviet-Polish War of 1920, the Molotov-Ribbentrop Pact, etc. This was an anti-Soviet stance, but it wasn't nationalistic chauvinism. We were simply telling the truth.

But today we're witnessing the degeneration of nationalism in Poland. Many of its current adherents are chauvinists. If their nationalism is anti-Putinist, very often it's also Russophobic by default. Jaroslaw Kaczyński has been backing the Ukrainians not because he's a Ukrainophile but because he's a Russophobe. He has no idea what Ukraine actually is. They're isolationists in their psychology. Their nationalism is not only anti-Ukrainian, anti-Semitic and anti-Russian, it's also anti-European. The extreme right had a slogan: "Liberals and pederasts are Euro-enthusiasts." They claim Poland should be taking its lead from the US, but the US is far away; our immediate neighbour is Germany, and that's who we need to engage with. But they didn't want to talk to the Germans. When the Kaczyńskis were in power [the first time], Polish-German relations were very bad. And this is the sort of nationalism that frightens me: it's Bolshevist in its psychology, chauvinist in its rhetoric and isolationist in terms of its programme. This would be curtains for Poland. You have to understand that Pushkin's Russia and Putin's Russia aren't the same thing. And cultural ties with Russia, Ukraine, Germany and France are only going to enrich us, we need to develop them.

Navalny We're seeing the same tendencies in today's Russia as well.

Michnik It's exactly the same psychology! I never believed Poland's accession to the EU would pose a risk to our identity, as our nationalists were claiming. It's nonsense! France is an EU member, but does that mean it's somehow ceased being France? Our nationalists were screaming about the murder of Polish sovereignty. But I know what it was really all about: just like Vladimir Vladimirovich, they were thinking, "we won't be able to do what we want in our country – we won't be able to jail our opponents," and so on, because of the EU and because of NATO, the two anchors of Polish democracy. Of course, they cannot fully guarantee its preservation, as the examples of Greece and Hungary demonstrate, but they're not insignificant either. And my Ukrainian colleagues know it. Entry into the European Union would ensure no new Yanukovych comes to power there.

Navalny But when the Kaczyńskis were in power the first time, why did they fail to establish an authoritarian regime?

Michnik Their own stupidity was to blame. Their Law and Justice party had entered into a coalition with the populist Self-Defence Party and the nationalist conservative League of Polish Families. In 2007 they fell out among themselves and launched a criminal case against Andrzej Lepper, the Self-Defence leader, accusing him of corruption.[68] Shortly before the early parliamentary elections, I was called in for questioning by the Łódź prosecutor. He offered to interrogate me off the record. I told him I was already a "criminal" when he was still a kindergartener, and that I knew these tricks like the back of my hand. I had nothing to say regarding the Lepper case. I was released but invited to come back a few days later, after the parliamentary elections. But as soon as it became clear the Kaczyńskis had lost, they called me up and told me the matter was closed and that I needn't come back in. Our democratic institutions had done their job and the Kaczyńskis' machinations had failed. And this is an obvious difference between Poland and Russia: in Poland we don't know who's going to be president until the last minute.

Navalny For me, the clearest demonstration of the success of Poland's democratic reforms can be found in the aftermath of the Smolensk presidential plane disaster.[69] Poland lost a substantial proportion of its political elite, including, of course, the president himself, but this didn't result in a political crisis or nationwide turmoil. In contrast, the "No Putin, No Russia" formula is being drilled into Russians' heads.

Michnik It was a terrible tragedy. Jaroslaw Kaczyński is still insisting it was a terrorist attack. That's nonsense. But that's the psychology of these people. It's high time their Law and Justice party was rechristened Suspiciousness and Fear. People often say nowadays that the government didn't do too well in that "exam." I don't agree.

In my opinion, everything's in order. Poland is a properly functioning state. Disasters do happen. We were afraid everything would take a turn for the worse, but things progressed in the right way: the early presidential elections were held as planned, there was a change of government. Our democratic institutions did their job, it's true.

Navalny And that's what Russia needs to strive towards, too. A country's strength doesn't stem from the fact that a Great Leader and Teacher is in charge – it stems from the fact that old leaders cede their office to new ones, which the country is constantly producing. In a normally functioning democracy you can get rid of three presidents in a row, and there'll still be new ones waiting in the wings. Of course, a catastrophe [like the Smolensk plane crash] puts tremendous stress on the country, but the political mechanisms go to work to ensure someone new takes the helm, and the system continues to function as normal. Now *that* is a true demonstration of the state's robustness.

Michnik What do you think would transpire if – God forbid! – something comparable were to happen in Russia?

Navalny That would create the potential for very dangerous scenarios, because the Kremlin is turning the "No Putin, No Russia" formula into reality. The system of governance is purposefully being made to revolve around a single person. But we're all mortals. Power verticals are very unstable structures that can collapse in a second and drag everything down with them. Destroying as they do all possible alternatives, authoritarian regimes leave behind a scorched earth. In my opinion, it's a great tragedy for Russia that we're even *discussing* the question of whether our country would survive Putin's departure. What utter nonsense! Russia's been around a millennium and we're wondering whether it'll survive beyond Putin!

Michnik The Chinese experiment is an interesting one. They've been able to create a mechanism for leadership change, but a non-democratic one.

Navalny Yes, the leadership changes every ten years, but power is never concentrated in the hands of a single person. The party has at least created a system for producing new leaders, so if something happens to the current one, we know there won't be any catastrophe. We're not talking elections here, of course, but it *is* a political compromise between broad interest groups. It's bulldogs fighting under a carpet, but they're keeping to a set of rules.

Michnik They've really done their homework on what happened in the Soviet Union and are doing their utmost to avoid the same mistakes.

Navalny It's curious that the Russian ruling elite is trying to present the Chinese way of doing things as an alternative point of reference for Russia. Coming from them, that's pretty funny. Firstly, because then there'd need to be a change of president every ten years, and secondly, because they'd all need to be shot. China has executed thousands of officials, including the highest-ranking ones, for corruption. So our own regime can't possibly hold China up as an example of the right way to go – otherwise they'd all need to commit suicide.

Michnik I think we just still know very little about China. And we can't yet see how their experiment is going to end.

Navalny Returning to the subject of post-Putin Russia, I'd say that Putin's departure won't be a full stop, for better or for worse. The question is what his departure's going to spark off. We can see, for example, that an Islamic state has been created in Chechnya, with the leader of that state publicly pledging fealty to Putin – and to Putin alone. We have to ask, then: what would Kadyrov and his army of fighters do if Putin wasn't there?

In the long term, the destruction of regionalism and the seizure of all power by Moscow could bring about the collapse of the state: the Moscow-installed governors could take advantage of the resulting power vacuum and tear the country apart. Putin's destruction of the system of checks and balances represents one of the gravest crimes he's committed against Russia.

I'm not a big fan of the federal system. I believe power should be devolved to an even lower level – that of urban authorities rather than regional ones. That's where three quarters of the population actually live. We need to redistribute power, to turn city mayors into the country's most powerful figures, and devolve funds and political authority to actual population centres.

Michnik I agree.

Navalny I think we could mend the situation by making use of your experience and creating – as far as our capabilities allow – parallel civil society structures that would allow us to intercept [unbridled] power. And by devising plans for future reforms right now.

Michnik That's very important! You need a fully-fledged project! We weren't quite ready to take power – it all happened so suddenly: in May '89 we were nowhere but, come August, Mazowiecki had already been appointed prime minister. We let the moment slip.

9

The Church and Fundamentalism

Navalny Since we've brought up Mazowiecki, it'd be very interesting to discuss the question of the interrelationship between church and state. We've already mentioned the Catholic Church and its political role on several occasions. As I understand it, the church in Poland seeks to use the state to reach its goals and to bring the state under its control, whereas in Russia it's predominantly the *state* that's using the church to *its* own ends. You said the church did a lot to restore Polish sovereignty, but then went as far as to demand special status for the Catholic religion in the Constitution. But it never fully succeeded in turning the state into its own instrument, did it?

Michnik It didn't, no. But the controversy still hasn't been fully resolved. There are two main aspects to the dispute: the question of ecclesiastical privileges and the question of the church's tangible influence on politics.[70] The former involves issues like taxation, funding, school education, restitution. In terms of politics, that's very precarious terrain. The majority of our bishops are convinced that since 90% of the Polish population are Catholics, the ruling regime should be Catholic as well. That's nonsense. President Bronislaw Komorowski may be a conservative Catholic but he understands that, first and foremost, he's the president of the country. There was a quarrel regarding the European convention against domestic violence:[71] the

Church was against the convention's ratification because it contains a definition of gender. The president then said, "I don't agree with the bishops and I'm going to sign this into law." Another dispute concerned in-vitro fertilisation (IVF). The church came out against it. But our president said that IVF wasn't abortion, and signed the bill into law because while abortion is the destruction of life, IVF allows life to be created. And it's good that this happened, because everyone then saw that the government was independent of the church. But that issue hasn't been fully resolved.

Navalny And does the church provide systematic support to any particular political force? It's obvious that Kaczyński must be more to the clerics' taste, but can any general stance be discerned?

Michnik There's no obvious one, because the church doesn't speak with a single voice either. There are various tendencies within it. But the majority support Kaczyński's Law and Justice Party, though not always publicly or openly. I think they're making a mistake – Kaczyński's no clericalist, he's a proponent of Gallicanism.[72] Yes, we might be a Catholic country, we've got our Catholic schools and our Catholic symbolism, but it's politicians rather than bishops who wield the real power. Kaczyński's simply using the church to his own political ends. But this problem can't be as serious in Russia as it is in Poland.

Navalny It's all completely different in Russia. For two hundred years the church was basically a special government agency. In Soviet times it was either persecuted or subordinated to the state. In Poland, the church tells the state what it should and shouldn't do, whereas the reverse is true in Russia. The patriarchate provides the state with ideological support.

Think back to the Pussy Riot affair; when it actually happened, almost nobody paid any attention to it.[73] But then the Kremlin issued a few instructions, and suddenly there was this huge brouhaha about offending believers' feelings.[74] And today it's clear that the church initially adopted a cautious stance vis-à-vis Ukraine and Crimea, before eventually backing the Kremlin.

Michnik And isn't the Moscow Patriarchate worried about the reaction of the Ukrainian Orthodox Church?

Navalny I think it is. A significant proportion of the ROC's [Russian Orthodox Church] parishes are on Ukrainian territory, and the congregations there are really large because the population's more religious. So Patriarch Kirill was treading very carefully at first, and for a while he completely disappeared from the public sphere. Even now the matter isn't discussed at the highest echelons, but at grassroots level we've seen a good many priests running around with machine guns and actively supporting the Kremlin's policies.

There's no unified attitude to the church in opposition circles, though many believe the ROC should remain a constant target of criticism. I'm a believer and rarely speak out on church-related issues, and, when I do, many of my colleagues argue I'm not being critical enough. It might seem paradoxical, but I'm for an expansion of the church's practical, tangible role in society, because right now, in my opinion, the church in Russia exists only on a symbolic level. You've got the recognisable churchly accoutrements, but the significance of it all – the inner meaning – is long since lost. People barely go to church. Easter services this year were attended by no more than 5% of Russians, while over 70% self-identify as Orthodox. I'd like the church to disseminate the basic ideas of Christianity more actively. It's high time we remembered what exactly its primary mission is: to spread the teachings of Jesus Christ. And the church should be encouraged in every possible way to do just that. So far, though, it's just the religion's external trappings that are proliferating in the country. In this regard, I – unlike the hierarchs of the Russian Orthodox Church – don't see any problem with a papal visit to Russia, because this would amplify society's interest in Christianity, and I don't believe it'd result in a mass exodus from Orthodoxy to Catholicism.[75] But when I express my thoughts on what the role of the church should be, people tell me that in practice the church isn't actually going to preach the ideas of Christ – the church is going to concern itself with land, property and the struggle for power. I think this is one of the challenges facing the new Russia: church must be separated from state, but suitable conditions must also be created for the church to propagate Christian ideas.

Michnik You had some wonderful priests. Father Aleksandr Men …

Navalny Yes, excellent example! And now there's Deacon Andrei Kuraev, who daringly gives vent to his opinions, which, on occasion, can be very oppositionist and liberal in character. But there are very few others like him. There's a certain degree of unrest within the church – perhaps even a significant one – but there's also military-style discipline. The top brass like to feel they're part of the state apparatus, and tolerate no divergence of opinions on political issues.

Michnik That's not the case in Poland, of course.

Navalny It's interesting that the traditional church in Russia doesn't act in the same way as churches in other countries that cast themselves as highly religious (Poland, the US, Latin American countries). In those places, the church launches direct attacks on society and makes specific demands: the prohibition of abortion, gay marriage, etc. Our problem is that it'd be good for the ROC to do just that. It'd be a positive thing for society as a whole if our church concerned itself with "traditional" problems, because this would serve to bring in the right kind of conservatism. Not concocted religious fundamentalism or the postmodern madness we witnessed during the Pussy Riot trial, but a healthy conservatism, which, though dangerous in large doses, by and large stabilises society because it's directed, for example, towards the preservation of the family.

Michnik I absolutely agree and, in general, my assessment of the role of the church is a positive one. I don't like the new wave of atheism amongst young people – it has a nihilistic character. I can't imagine my country without the Catholic Church, that's just impossible. The only question is this: what sort of character will this church have, exactly, and what's going to be its relationship with politics, nationalism and chauvinism? I'm a Pole and a Catholic so I understand how this all came about. In the nineteenth century, the western regions of Poland were ruled over by Protestant Prussians, while Orthodox Russians ruled the east. The Poles sensed the threat to their church and looked to Catholicism for the foundations of their identity. During the communist dictatorship, the church was frequently the people's only refuge. But lots of things have changed now and there's no threat to speak of, yet individual bishops are claiming the current liberal regime wants the "biological extermination of the Polish people." What nonsense!

Navalny Now in this case there really are parallels with Russia. There's no need for any intervention into politics, just into the spiritual realm. Sermonising's all very well and good, but trying to influence politicians directly is completely unacceptable.

Michnik But there are other bishops and priests in Poland as well, which is why I consider myself a friend of the church. But that's not how I'm seen by the majority of bishops.

Navalny The patriarchate of Alexy II differed stylistically – and for the better – from that of Kirill. The political context was different as well. Kirill can be regarded as Putin's creation. Putin needed a militant church leader – one prepared to parrot whatever words he might want him to parrot, and to create a fundamentalist myth.

Michnik In 2012, Patriarch Kirill and Archbishop Jozef Michalik delivered a joint appeal of reconciliation to the nations of Poland and Russia.[76] On the one hand, this nascent dialogue between the Polish Catholic priests and their Russian Orthodox counterparts represents a positive development, serving as it does to overcome the Russophobia and Polonophobia in our respective countries. On the other hand, though, it could degenerate into a coalition against liberal European values. The current Catholic Church in Poland is not the church of Wojtyla [Pope John Paul II]. And our bishops really don't like Pope Francis.

Navalny I think the Catholic *nomenklatura* around the world aren't particularly fond of him – he's too much of an ascetic.

Michnik The 70s, I think, witnessed a certain resurgence of religion among the Russian intelligentsia. And what happened subsequently?

Navalny This might have been to do with the dissident movement: in the eyes of the state, all otherwise-minded people – including religious activists – were now being equated with dissidents. There was a point when the regime began to repress everyone. Alexander Podrabinek writes in his book[77] about a family jailed because they set up a printing works that they used to publish religious literature. So I don't think we're really talking a mass intellectual-class return to the churchly fold here. People just ended up in the same boat – in the same jail cell, that is: some for *The Gulag Archipelago*, and others for the Bible.

Michnik Yes, I understand. But there were these symbolic figures: Solzhenitsyn, Maximov, Sinyavsky. They all embraced religion.

Navalny Perhaps. But I don't think all of them embraced the official form of Orthodoxy. In Russia, there was something of a religious revival in the early twentieth century, but it took on unorthodox forms.[78] The intelligentsia developed quite a thing for God-seeking, while Old Belief and sectarianism enjoyed the widest degree of popularity amongst the masses. In the late Soviet period, meanwhile, Anabaptism became relatively widespread. There were people who wanted to embrace God, but not through the official church. We can observe the same thing happening in China: not only is Christianity on the rise there, but local sectarianism – Falun Gong – has also emerged. In a sense, this too represents a kind of refuge from the omnipresent state.

Michnik I don't think that anything's possible without religion. I once wrote that the collapse of the Catholic Church would open the door to nihilism. But many of our bishops are doing everything they possibly can to bring about just that, discrediting the church in the process. I was recently invited to take part in a discussion with the senior bishops of our church for the first time in twenty-five years. I was invited on the insistence of a Vatican cardinal. Let's see how the situation will continue to pan out. I'm not too optimistic about it. But I had the same attitude to the new pope, and he turned out to be a very wise man.

Navalny There've been big contemporary art-related scandals involving the church in Poland too, haven't there?

Michnik We've had more than our fair share.[79] But, you know, I wasn't a fan of what Pussy Riot did either. Had this happened in Poland, not only would I not have supported their actions, I would've condemned them. We must, after all, make a distinction between *sacrum* and *profanum*, holy and worldly. I do understand the substance of their political pronouncements, but the form they were couched in is alien to me. In my newspaper I frequently criticise the bishops myself, but I never speak out against the church as an institution, nor against religion as a whole. But sending those girls off to that labour colony was, of course, going too far.

Navalny I agree. It was an instance of petty hooliganism, and it would've sufficed just to issue a fine. And this represents a very important issue for me. It's currently being instilled in us that Russia – in contrast to Europe, with its cosmopolitan liberalism and gay-pride parades – is a country of traditional values. But what do we actually see?

Poland's a European country, and one that's really way more traditional than contemporary Russia. More than a third of the population regularly go to church, unlike our paltry 3-4%! This is yet another one of Putin's mythologems: the Kremlin has created this myth about the conservatism of the Russian people, and an Iranian-style administration of justice is the natural upshot of this. Recently, a group of girls were arrested in Russia for dancing at the Malaya Zemlya memorial in Novorossiysk.[80] It was hard to imagine something like that happening even in Soviet times.

As far as I understand it, abortion is still banned in Poland?

Michnik Not in all cases, but it's largely illegal, yes. It's a subject of fervent public debate.

Navalny Russia, on the other hand, has the highest number of abortions per woman in the world! Those liberal Europeans with loose morals have a long way to go before they can catch up with us! And there's the peculiarity of Russia: it's not so much a case of a confrontation between the modernised and traditional strata of society, as it is a case of the Kremlin feeding the public myths about a deeply entrenched Russian traditionalism. Putin's ideology is strikingly eclectic: it encompasses everything from Stalin to the church. It's funny to watch all these erstwhile KGB and Komsomol members strutting around churches with candles in hand. Unlike the Poles, they were all atheists in Soviet times.

Michnik And Putin's right there himself!

Navalny When I was three years old, my grandmother arranged for me to be christened while staying with some relatives in Ukraine. She kept this a secret from my father because he was a communist. They were afraid he'd be expelled from the Communist party. By historical standards, this happened virtually yesterday, and now it turns out that those self-same committed Soviet communists are the most religious people of all, and they're criticising me for spreading liberal ideas in our conservative society. This really makes me laugh!

Michnik Yes, that's true.

Navalny But it's not really obvious how we go about fighting this myth. All of a sudden us Russians are Eurasia's foremost fundamentalists!

Michnik The far right in France, Italy and Germany are now gazing over at Moscow with a great deal of respect …[81]

Navalny And here's another astounding turn of events – for me, the political love affair between Putin and Marine Le Pen is the very height of postmodernism! No other two politicians anywhere in the world disagree to such an extent on fundamental policy issues: while Marine Le Pen speaks out against migrants, Putin opposes any visa regime with the countries of Central Asia; Marine Le Pen is against Islamic fundamentalism, while certain regions of Russia are now practically under Sharia law. But, in spite of everything, these people are friends! I don't really understand how this can be.

Michnik They are united by their hatred of democracy, tolerance and pluralism. Despite the ideological differences between Nazism and Communism, the two regimes were very similar. Hitler's diplomats even noted in 1939 that their stay in Moscow had felt like calling in at an old friend's. Stalin applauded when Hitler killed Röhm.[82] As the French say, *les extrêmes se touchent* [extremes converge]. Ten years ago people in Russia were telling me that Putin was a Westernist. Later, in Warsaw, Nikita Petrov said to me, "Yes, Putin's indeed a Westernist. Because, for him, the GDR is the West as well."

Navalny What Putin's creating here really is reminiscent of the GDR in some ways. In its fundamentals, his "sovereign democracy" is similar to Stalin's "people's democracy."[83] These are varieties of imitation democracy.[84] He's constructing an improved, East German-style version of the Soviet Union. Yes, some don't like what he's doing, and some are fleeing across the border, but the majority seem to be satisfied with everything.

Michnik And he's letting people leave – that's the thing.

Navalny He's drawn some conclusions from the tragic Soviet experience. Back then no one was allowed to leave, and a critical mass of disgruntled people accumulated within the country. This is no longer the case. But, in its essence, the social contract hasn't changed too much since those days: you can prosper as long as you waive your political rights. We'll keep you fed and watered, and you'll put up with us. And now there's the added opportunity of going abroad and spending money there. Their monopoly on power is now served with a slightly different ideological sauce: back then, we were building the most progressive regime in the history of the world, whereas now they're telling us that the Russian people simply can't live any other way – we've the mentality of slaves, and our love for the whip is genetically ingrained. They're very fond of Pushkin's quip that "the government is the sole European in Russia." Perhaps this really was true in Pushkin's day, but it isn't true now. I think it's an insult to the Russian people.

Michnik Absolutely! The same thing happened in Poland as well. Under communism people would privately say, "What do you want? Freedom and democracy? But then you'll get anti-Semitic pogroms! No freedom for the Poles!" It's twenty-five years later and there's hasn't been a single pogrom – not even an anti-Soviet one!

In the late nineteenth century there was a very widespread view that the Poles simply couldn't have their own sovereign statehood. And it wasn't only anarchists who said it. I've read interrogation documents from the January Uprising of 1863.[85] Oskar Awejde, a member of the clandestine government, wrote a lengthy book in his prison cell where he argued that democracy was an absolute no-no for the Poles, that the Poles weren't even a nation-state. And now it's obvious to everybody that, while Poland may have a variety of traditions – some good, some bad – the thesis that Poles simply can't do without dictatorship is utter drivel. Just like the thesis that Russians aren't keen on democracy.

Navalny This is one of my main motivations – to prove that the Russian people are no less well adapted to democracy than any other nation. The government hates the Russian people and is instilling them with a slave mentality. It's a national tragedy, but many people actually take pleasure in it – it's giving rise to a kind of Stockholm syndrome. It's interesting to hear you've already been through this. How do we surmount it?

Michnik First of all you need to tell the truth – to explain that state propaganda distorts historical facts and that such proclamations, even if made in veiled form, serve to violate Russia's national honour. Secondly, cultural exchange is of critical importance – Russians need to be closely familiarised with the European way of life. Here's one very good example. The Kaliningrad region and Poland have a visa-free travel agreement, and it's a region that's been open to Europe for a very long time.[86] The people there are totally European now – a lot of things have changed; Kaliningrad residents are real Russians, but in large part Europeanised ones. And there, civic solidarity – the foundation of all democratic foundations – is gradually materialising.

Navalny That really is a good example! This is a region that has closer links to Europe – a whole order of magnitude closer, in fact – than any other, and yet nothing terrible has happened: there are no weekly gay-pride parades, the traditional family hasn't been destroyed, and not an inch of Russian soil has been stolen by those "dreadful" Europeans. An excellent example!

10

The Path to Europe

Navalny Together with Václav Havel, you're regarded as the co-originator of the idea of a "return to Europe." Could you tell me about this in a little more detail?[87]

Michnik We knew we needed to get away from the Soviet Union – the further away the better. And if that's impossible in a geographical sense, you need to make it happen on a cultural level. We were well aware a distinction had to be made between Soviet and Russian culture. Real Russian culture inspired many of us in our anti-Soviet endeavours; for example, it was Jerzy Giedroyc – a *Pole* rather than an American or a Frenchman – who first published the work of Sinyavsky and Daniel.

There were exceptions, of course. Milan Kundera believed Russian culture to be alien to Europe, and had a very negative attitude to Dostoevsky, for example – hence his famous polemic with Joseph Brodsky.[88] In political terms, I agree with Kundera, who believed that the Soviet Union had taken Eastern Europe hostage, but, culturally speaking, I fully side with Brodsky.

When this idea of a "return" was being formulated in the 1970s and 1980s, we naturally didn't know what'd happen next, but we realised that, should some critical juncture arrive, we'd need to know how to behave. We could see that the European Community was a guarantor of democratic order, human rights, freedom of speech, an uncensored media environment, open borders, and so forth. And, in order to conform to its norms, it was necessary to renounce Polish messianism and national chauvinism. After all, European values entail maintaining good relations with your neighbours and with national minorities. The return to Europe was a return to a normal government, to democracy, to a tolerant political society, to the rule of law. Europe was a refuge from our domestic hell. Many of us were afraid of "sovereign democracy" in the Putinist sense of the term. In 1968, I saw anti-Semitism gaining momentum under the influence of propaganda. And I was afraid of a hysterical chauvinist Polish horde.

I know that Russia's currently debating whether to strike an article from the Constitution that gives priority to the norms of international law.

Navalny For the Putin regime, this issue[89] is an entirely practical one. He's constantly losing cases in the European Court of Human Rights (ECHR). He therefore needs to make it so the Court can't overrule Russian decisions, hence his periodic warnings that Russia may withdraw from the ECHR's jurisdiction. I've won cases in the European Court myself, as have the Yukos shareholders. Russia's ranked first in the world in terms of the number of complaints filed with the court. An interesting situation is developing: tens of thousands of people across the country regard the ECHR as the only place where they can get justice. My position on this issue is therefore unequivocal – international law should prevail over national legislation. We were the ones who agreed to and signed these conventions.

Michnik Spot on. In Poland, of course, we had our own internal debates about Europe, and many radicals, both on the far right and the far left, were against joining the EU.

The far left said it was just a bourgeois capitalist project. The far right claimed EU membership meant the end of Polish sovereignty – that we'd fought for independence and now Poland would be sold off to foreign corporations and so on. But we won. And today no serious person would ever say we need to leave the European Union. It's obvious now we shouldn't.

Navalny It's interesting that there was a debate around the issue in Poland as well, with some people even continuing to challenge the correctness of the decision. Sometimes these debates seem very odd to me. I believe the time has come for Russia to definitively recognise itself as a part of Europe. And it's high time discussions about Russia's "special path" – which took their rise from the Slavophile-Westerniser debates and have remained at the heart of Russian philosophy for two hundred years – were consigned to the past.[90]

Michnik In Germany, too, people speculated for ages about the *deutscher Sonderweg* [the German special path]...[91]

Navalny And there was a similar phenomenon in Spain as well. Many countries have been through this. In my opinion, though, the history of the last century has clearly demonstrated that all projects save for the European are unsustainable. And countries pursuing their own "special path" have ultimately arrived at some flavour or other of totalitarianism. Our westernised elite has systematically deceived the population by instilling this "special path" idea into people's minds. No special path actually exists.

Michnik Do you think, for example, that the Great Reforms of Alexander II were a lie?[92]

Navalny They were enforced steps in the right direction. The elite was well aware there could be no normal life, no normal development, without the inauguration of European-style institutions. As a result we ended up getting a perfectly civilised legal system, for example. Whatever rhetoric may have accompanied it, this was a movement down that selfsame European path. But it wasn't consistent enough, which is why we witnessed the collapse of our special-way-seeking state on two occasions during the twentieth century. And if we don't put ourselves firmly on track for Europe we're going to see a third collapse as well. Even after one and a half years of intensive anti-European propaganda, the level of support for a European path of development in Russia hasn't fallen below 30%. Before the onset of the Putinist hysteria, it was invariably at the 50% mark. If you offer any Russian – whether a Kaliningrader, Vladivostokian or a native of anywhere in between – a choice between the Chinese, Singaporean or European models of state-society relations, they're always going to plump for the latter. Because everyone thinks trials should be fair and independent. That's what Russians regard as the norm.

Michnik It's just that you shouldn't call it the European path – you should say it's the Russian path.

Navalny I don't think there's any contradiction between the two.

Michnik Yes, but when you tell folk from the provinces about the "European path," they don't quite get what this means.

Navalny That's absolutely true, especially after prolonged exposure to propaganda. A catastrophic equivocation has taken place. When we mention "the European way," the response is, "Oh, we get it – same-sex marriage and gay-pride parades." But if we ask whether people want their town's mayor to depend on their own will or the Kremlin's, well, the answer's totally obvious. Same thing with the courts system. We're perfectly aware of the fact Russia has always had a special status within Europe because Russia's a very large country. Then again, Poland occupies a special position as well. There were fears, after all, that Poland would be too big for the EU. And many European politicians still believe that Poland's political role within the EU is incommensurate with its economic role. Russia, meanwhile, has almost four times Poland's population, so if we assume that the current EU administration system and the European Parliament's population-based seat allocation system remain in place, and Russia accedes under the same conditions as other member states, its role would be simply immense, resulting in the transformation of the entire EU. We realise there are many misgivings in this regard and that many Europeans would be less than happy for Russia to join on an equal footing. Technical issues are up for discussion. But not the general question. Russia's future is in Europe alone. No regime other than one founded on the basic rules of European democracy is going to be sustainable. It'd survive only by means of censorship, repression and fraud.

Michnik Russia is a very large country, and I can imagine that it'd even be too big for the EU. But the US is big too. And if Russia-EU relations were comparable to EU-US relations, characterised by common values, open borders and excellent economic cooperation, there'd be no problems to speak of.

Navalny In your opinion, Adam, does Russia have a place

to "return" to? Do you consider Russia a part of Europe in civilisational terms?

Michnik Of course! How could you even imagine European culture without the likes of Pushkin, Gogol, Tolstoy, Turgenev, Chekhov, Tchaikovsky, Stravinsky and others? That's just impossible! There's no European culture without them! In Poland they compiled a list of the greatest books of the twentieth century. First place went to Mikhail Bulgakov's novel *The Master and Margarita*, and works by other Russian writers also made the top ten. We were publishing Russian literature even while operating underground, despite the fact that this could land us in jail. And this is to say nothing of Russia's visual arts tradition, its cinema, its science! It's odd that this question even exists in Russia; that the subject's even debated.

There are myths of this kind in all sorts of countries – in Germany, Poland, Spain, Scandinavia. But Russia's contribution to European culture is obvious!

Navalny Yes, and as I've already mentioned, the cultural sphere's a very organic space for us to expand in. Disney generated nearly $50 billion in revenue last year, while Russia made less than $10 billion from arms exports, even though we're very proud of our military-industrial sector. Culture, science, education, these are all areas we can make huge money from while simultaneously remaining on excellent terms with the outside world. Instead of continuing to close ourselves off from Europe we should be doing the opposite!

Michnik Absolutely. And what's your view on Poland?

Navalny Poland has a very particular significance in

Russian eyes – it's a country Russians aren't indifferent to. There are long-established, stable stereotypes of Poland and Poles in Russia, and various manifestations of these stereotypes.[93] In Soviet times, for example, "national" jokes were very common. And there was a whole series of jokes involving a Russian, a German and a Pole. Three people; three different worldviews; three models of behaviour – very symbolic. Polish cinema enjoyed enormous popularity in the Soviet Union. When I was a kid, incidentally, I read Przymanowski's Four Tank-Men and a Dog many times over. He must've been regarded as a Soviet collaborator in Poland?

Michnik Exactly. Fourth-rate writer. I knew him personally. A blatant lackey of the regime. You should've heard the things he said about Solidarity during martial law! He accused us of wanting to slaughter all the communists! Utter lunacy!

Navalny Crazy stuff. My whole childhood was punctuated by these Polish names: Gustlik, Janek[94] ... Returning to the subject, though, Russia's relations with Poland go back such a long way and have been intense enough to've left a mark even on popular consciousness. Naturally, there's a predominance of negative stereotypes that populist politicians love to exploit. The notion of the cunning, treacherous, Russian-hating Pole is a very common one in Russia. The normalisation of relations with Poland is, I think, one of the most complex and pressing challenges facing the new Russia. We should be learning from Poland – the problems Poland confronted on its path to Europe will be our problems, too. I've seen lots of European anti-Polish posters focusing on labour migration, for example. We all remember the French "Polish plumber" meme.[95] When Russia moves closer to

Europe it'll encounter the exact same problems. Open borders will also generate a westward torrent of migrants. We're going to go down the same path and we're going to use the Polish experience as a point of reference along the way.

And there's another aspect to consider. I think we need to draw a definitive line under the history of our relations. Yes, they haven't been easy, but you need to keep history and politics separate and make sure they don't mix too much. History's very important and it's not a question of forgetting everything. But these are still different discourses we're talking about, after all. I understand that it's difficult. I hope to get a full sense of the tragedy that the massacre of almost 22,000 Polish officers in the Katyn forest, and in the Starobelsk and Ostashkov camps,[96] represented for the Polish nation. This crime of Stalin's claimed the nation's bloom. And it was an absolutely correct, if belated, step for Russia to recognise its guilt in this crime. But I'd like the Poles to go a little easier on those among my compatriots who still don't understand what happened, and who can sometimes be aggressive in their response when reminded of this tragedy. Our nation hasn't yet fully grasped the sheer scale of Stalin's repressions, hasn't realised that Stalin, along with Hitler, was the chief executioner of the Russian people.

Michnik I understand. Katyn's just a drop of blood in the ocean of Stalinist repressions.

Navalny This has yet to be comprehended fully. And I know how reverent the Polish attitude is to the Warsaw Uprising of 1944,[97] about which almost nothing is known in Russia. The reaction you get from most Russians goes something like this: "Get off our case, okay? We lost 27 million people, we liberated you from the fascists, and you're pestering us about officers and revolts and what have you!" This is the wrong approach, without any doubt. It has to give way to a more complex, more sympathetic attitude. But I don't think this is for politicians to get involved with. The best thing they can do is to open the archives and create maximally favourable conditions for the work of historians and social organisations from both countries. And at some point things really were moving in that direction. Officially in Russia there's no question mark over who shot the Polish officers in 1940. We've acknowledged our culpability.

Michnik That's the crucial thing – without an admission of guilt, dialogue would be impossible.

Navalny There's an absolutely fantastic Katyn Memorial.

Michnik That's right.

Navalny And we saw how positively Polish society reacted when classified documents from Russian archives were handed over in 2010, and Putin publicly expressed his regret. Here you have to give him credit.

Michnik But Yeltsin, it has to be said, was the first to do this. I agree that for the majority of Russians, Katyn and the Warsaw Uprising are individual details in the vast expanse of war. You'll get the same reaction from Ukrainians if you ask them about the Volhynia massacres.[98] Russia, just like Ukraine, is a very large, very diverse country. There's no single, uniform Russia, no single Ukraine. I told Yushchenko his main mistake wasn't so much making Bandera a national hero as the fact he didn't bestow that status on anyone else. Why not make a hero, for example, of Pyotr Grigorenko, the Red Army general and dissident? It has to be understood that making Bandera out to be the sole founder of the new Ukraine is a mistake. Yes, he's a complex figure in a complex historical context but, ideologically speaking, he was a Ukrainian fascist! We have to speak the truth.

Navalny There's another problematic aspect to our bilateral relations: Poland's NATO membership and the expansion of the missile defence programme.

Michnik I remember how Mikhail Gorbachev, an absolute opponent of NATO expansion, came over to Poland, and told our president, Aleksander Kwaśniewski, that Poland's membership of the Alliance was a mistake. Kwaśniewski asked him what he thought of Yeltsin. And when Gorbachev responded by calling Yeltsin a fool and a drunkard, Kwaśniewski asked how he could possibly fail to join NATO if a nuclear power had this kind of president! NATO membership was, I believe, one more step in the direction of the Western world for us. And now, looking on at what's happening with Ukraine, I'm happy that we're in NATO. Kuchma gave up Ukraine's nuclear weapons in exchange for guarantees regarding the inviolability of his country's borders. Russia made these guarantees but didn't fulfil them. I'm no militarist and believe that war invariably represents the defeat of politics. But, given the current situation, NATO is the only guarantor of Poland's security.

Navalny I believe every country can choose for itself whether to join NATO or not. The problem as I see it isn't NATO membership *per se* but the expansion of the missile defence programme. Nuclear parity (the doctrine of mutual assured destruction) has been an important component of the international security system. Its violation is pushing

Russia into an arms race, which is something we really don't need.

Michnik I disagree. I believe that, should Russia become a democratic country, no NATO missiles are going to be a threat to it. No one in NATO or the EU wants a foot of Russian land.

Navalny I don't dispute that. It's absurd to hold guns to each others heads and call it security. But there's always the context to consider. We lived half a century under the doctrine of nuclear parity, everything's structured with a view to maintaining it. You can't just give it up tomorrow – not even if Russia's most liberal politicians were to triumph in the elections. It's a protracted process – not only do you need the political will to be forthcoming from both sides, you need a balanced point of departure. Parity represents precisely that. And then there'll be a lengthy period of give-and-take regarding disarmament. In the long term, I think, we should be aiming to establish a common defence system designed to counteract international terrorism, particularly of the Islamist variety.

Michnik Yes, we need a Russia-West alliance against threats of that kind. I'd hoped that things would evolve in that direction after 9/11, what with Putin being the first leader to call George W. Bush. I don't think there were any sentiments to suggest otherwise at the time.

Navalny That's the way things really were going, but at some point an obstacle of a subjective nature arose: Putin needed to consolidate his own power. And foreign policy then became an instrument for internal political manipulation, a tool he's been using to hold on to power. As the war with Ukraine testifies.

Michnik Absolutely.

Navalny And yet [Foreign Minister] Lavrov has said, quite rightly, that the main threat to Russia is ISIS. You can't argue with that. And this threat is a common one. But state propaganda has been inflating the threat posed by NATO, which isn't in the least relevant for Russia.

Michnik I agree. Which is why I've been saying that if a liberal-democratic government comes to power, it'll be a game-changer for Russia-West relations. No doubt you really do need to understand the mood of the people, their feelings and emotions, but at the same time you need to strive towards a goal. Of course, this doesn't mean you have to lie and say everything's going to be transformed overnight. But I think Russia's goal politically should be precisely that: an alliance with Europe and the US against international terrorism.

Navalny I agree. Russia should be integrated into a process initiated in Western Europe in the wake of the Second World War. Europe has to become a war-free zone. And this should become a priority.

11

Russia and Ukraine

Michnik It was Putin who unleashed the war, not the Europeans.

Navalny Precisely. It's a crime against the whole world, Russia included. Europe and Russia are home to around 800 million people, and these people deserve peace. I understand the Europeans, they're in shock because Russian-made anti-aircraft missiles are bringing down passenger aircraft.[99] It's unacceptable. Waging war to gain spheres of influence is an anachronism.

Michnik Clearly so.

Navalny The challenges today are completely different, which is why we have a long road of gradual reciprocal concessions ahead of us. We need a genuine reset of relations.

Michnik Everything currently depends on Russia and on its policies in Ukraine. Absolutely everything. In Poland there was a desire for a "reset." Komorowski, Tusk and Sikorski did a lot to get dialogue back on track. And now they're reproaching themselves for being too trusting of Putin. I'll do everything to bolster the Polish-Russian friendship. But I'm sure this is an impossibility under Putin, because I cannot convince the Poles that we need to change our policy towards a Russia that's holding my friends prisoner and waging war on Ukraine. This is absolutely unacceptable. As long as this authoritarian politics continues to develop, there'll be no improvement in relations between Russia and Poland. But this doesn't mean we shouldn't be bolstering cooperation between Russian and Polish democrats. We've done a lot towards this end; we invite our Russian friends to Poland and publish their works. We don't agree with the thesis that Russia means Putin. I've argued about this with Professor Richard Pipes. He was convinced that since Putin enjoys the support of 80% of the population, Russia can be equated with him. But I explained to him that the remaining 20% amounts to millions of people, which amounts to a massive potential for Russian democracy. Why am I obliged to regard Putin – or Brezhnev, for that matter – as the incarnation of Russia? Why not Sakharov? But while Putin remains in power there can be no progress. And I'm in favour of sanctions.

Navalny It has to be admitted that the sanctions, especially the sectoral sanctions, have done their job. As a citizen of Russia, I cannot endorse them and call for those particular sanctions to be expanded, but it'd be silly to deny it.

Michnik But as a citizen of Russia you can say that the regime is responsible for this state of affairs.

Navalny Undoubtedly so. But I believe the sanctions should be expanded in a different direction. It's imperative sanctions are imposed against "the party of war" – that is, the people responsible for the militaristic hysteria in Russia. So far, visa restrictions have been imposed on certain individuals in Putin's inner circle, but that's not enough. There are about a thousand people involved in the dissemination of war propaganda and hatred, and it's these people that must be shut off from Europe and the USA. The main beneficiaries of the war in Ukraine are not the military or even the imperial-leaning politicians; its main beneficiaries are the propagandists. We're well aware of the fact that these people aren't journalists. They just hide behind their press cards. They're the regime's media lackeys. And the only place that's truly sacred for them isn't Crimea, contrary to what Putin might say, but Europe and the US, where they go to spend the money they've earned here. They need to be denied the opportunity to do so. Europe, it would seem, is afraid of a counter-volley, but I suppose that's the price they're going to have to pay.

As long as Russia continues to fan the flames of war in eastern Ukraine, nothing will move forward. In fact, this war has hurt Russia no less than it's hurt Ukraine itself. We've fallen out with the entire civilised world and have paid dearly for it. And we've not finished paying for it either.

Michnik I keep saying that the war in Ukraine is a tragedy for Russia.

Navalny It's a terrible blow to Russia's long-term interests. And a blow, too, to the "Russian world" Putin's allegedly defending. There's no nation closer to Russia than the Ukrainians. And now the forty-million-strong Ukrainian nation will come to hate us. This shall never be erased from their collective memory. Generations will come and go, but the memory shall remain. And now, unfortunately, there's little that can be fixed. First of all, of course, we must stop the war and the destabilisation of Ukraine. And we have to admit the obvious: if Russia does have interests in Ukraine, those interests entail having a flourishing, developing neighbour with a successfully implemented democracy and general prosperity. Then things would return to normalcy.

Michnik And, of course, they also entail that all Russians living in Ukraine retain their rights, language and culture. Bilingualism presents no problem whatever. I think there won't be any issues as long as Poroshenko and Yatsenyuk remain in power. But Ukraine has its own Zhirinovskys. So anything is possible.

Navalny And Russia's currently doing everything to bring that notional Ukrainian Zhirinovsky to power. As long as the armed conflict continues, Russophobia and an anti-Russian stance will be popular among voters. And the larger-scale the conflict, the more popular they'll become.

Michnik Yes. That's a misfortune.

Navalny These tendencies have become more prominent in Poland, the Baltic States, Belarus, Moldova and even Kazakhstan. Everywhere, in fact. All the legends fabricated by the Kremlin, the "Russian world" and what have you, they've all been destroyed. Everything's fallen apart and we've nothing to show for it. We've paid for it all with sanctions and falling living standards. It's the second time the Russian people have been sold the idea of giving up a normal life for the sake of a completely idiotic and useless confrontation with the West. This is a problem of colossal proportions, and one we have to speak completely openly about. We have to end the war: on this our positions are identical. But here's what's interesting: Polish-Ukrainian relations have never been simple either. Yet we see today that the Poles fully support Ukraine. How did this come about?

Michnik Just like Poland, Ukraine underwent a process of Russification in the nineteenth century. So I know exactly where this anti-Russian syndrome among Ukrainians comes from.

If we consider Polish-Ukrainian relations, it's clear they've been beset by a multitude of problems. For a long time both the Poles and the Russians disputed the territory of Ukraine. The Poles said Ukraine was Poland, while the Russians claimed it for Russia. And no one would recognise Ukraine as Ukraine. The last time we did this was in 1920.[100] Poland took Galicia and Volhynia while Soviet Russia took everything else – a de facto division of Ukraine by Warsaw and Moscow. The Second World War made things yet more complex. The Volhynia massacres generated a victim complex among the Poles. After the war, Jerzy Giedroyc, the editor of the émigré journal *Kultura*, began to instil a new vision of Ukraine into Polish minds – Ukraine as the independent state of the Ukrainian nation.[101] In the 1970s I met Giedroyc in Paris and just couldn't understand – what was this Ukraine he was talking about? Ukraine, after all, was the USSR, i.e. Russia. But he'd already glimpsed another world and wasn't afraid to go against all the Polish myths: Russophobia, Ukrainophobia, anti-Semitism, imperial Jagiellonianism.[102] We gradually began to understand why it was so important to support Ukraine. But we never did so using the language of anti-Russian enmity!

There'd been many "black pages" in the history of Polish-Ukrainian relations, but we realised we needed to turn over a new leaf. Of course, you should always tell the truth, no matter how difficult this may be. I was once told by Bronislaw Geremek, who was already foreign minister at the time, "I find it easier to give a man a medal than to tell the truth." Now I recognise he was right. (By the way, Geremek was born in Minsk before moving to Lvov and later to Vilnius.) But we knew what we were aiming for.[103] In 1944, no one could have imagined that France and

Germany would ever enter into such a firm alliance, that there'd ever be any cooperation between them, but that's exactly what they achieved. And so will we.

Navalny The curious thing is that you managed to overcome the emotional upheavals regarding, for example, Vilnius and Lvov. After all, Vilnius was an absolutely Polish city in the first half of the twentieth century.[104]

Michnik Vilnius is the city of Mickiewicz and Pilsudski. And Lvov was a Polish city too. My father was born in Lvov.

Navalny And you were able to let them go.

Michnik I have to mention that the Poles have a very wise saying: you don't need to fight for territory or redraw any borders – what you need to do is open them up. If a Pole today wants to go to Vilnius, all he's got to do is board a train or get in his car. Because the border doesn't exist for him. And my dream is for people to be able to get to Kaliningrad or Moscow in the same way. I was once invited to a conference in Kaliningrad and it took two minutes to cross the border. This is what we should be striving towards – we shouldn't be looking to redraw any borders.

You've got to be able to accept reality. It's a question of making rational choices. Giedroyc explained to us that the Ukrainians and Lithuanians were established nations, each with their own country. Despite all the difficulties that may have existed between us in the past, we need to learn to respect each other and live in peace. I recently debated the subject of the Volhynia massacres with a Ukrainian nationalist. And one argument of his seemed convincing to me: Yes, these terrible murders took place, but they took place on Ukrainian soil. The Ukrainians didn't head to

Warsaw or Krakow to massacre the Poles there. This is in no way a justification of those barbaric murders, but there's something to ponder here. They wanted to live on their own land – something the Poles couldn't understand because they still regarded Volhynia as part of Poland. Only a newer generation came to understand that this was no longer the case.

Navalny I recently visited my brother in prison and passed through the Moscow, Kaluga, Bryansk and Orel regions on the way. This is the most densely populated part of Russia. But, passing through it, you get the impression that no one lives there at all. That it's a nature reserve. How can the thought of imperialism or external expansion even occur to us when there's virtually no one living here in European Russia? And that's to say nothing of Siberia and the Far East. Every last penny of budgetary funds should be poured into the development of lands we've already got!

As ideas go, imperialism is the most noxious one of all for the Russian people. It destroys all life and inhibits normal development. We deserve a normal life – proper education, proper medicine, proper roads. It's not war we need to invest in – it's human capital. Arriving in Europe, all Russians say, "I want to live like they do here – I want the courteous cops and the quality roads." But this is something we can achieve only by reforming Russia, not by seizing Ukraine and the Baltics. And the Russian people know this only too well. But the idea of external expansion is being aggressively drilled into their heads.

When TV stations scream all day long about how Ukrainian fascists are murdering Russians and crucifying children,[105] there's only one way people can react. It's an absolute nightmare. The brazenness of their propagandist lies is so off-the-scale that it's impossible to believe they actually are lies. It's the old Nazi principle: the more egregious the lie, the more truthful it appears. So I find it difficult to blame people who believe these barefaced falsehoods.

Michnik I've watched Russian TV – it's horrific.

Navalny I spent a year under house arrest and watched a lot of TV as a result. If I hadn't seen it with my own eyes, I wouldn't have believed you could ever actually hear a weather forecaster (!) say, "Things are heating up down Luhansk way, fighting's raging there – and the temperature's rising to boot."

I think Russians are absolutely prepared to make that rational choice you were talking about and recognise the Ukrainian state as a political entity. I know many questions arise in Europe when I call the Ukrainians a brother nation. I really do think that's the case. But that doesn't imply that I consider Ukrainians to be a particular subset of Russians or that I'm denying the Ukrainian nation's status as a political entity. It's just that we've a lot in common, and that's a good thing. And I don't think Russians' historical memory played any particular role in the annexation of the Crimea. I'm sure if you ask the average Russian you'll most probably find he's not read Tolstoy's *Sevastopol Stories* – unless of course he was a top-drawer literature student. But he certainly will react to the whole "fascists are killing Russians" thing. The problem of Crimea hasn't occupied anything remotely approaching a prominent position in Russian public policy for nearly a quarter-century. It was created artificially.

Michnik I think the only correct way to resolve the Crimea issue is to hold a referendum under international supervision. And I'd even admit the possibility of such a referendum in the Donbas. If they want to join Russia, let them do so. If they want independence, they can have that too.

Navalny Your point of view would be very unpopular in Ukraine.

Michnik But that's what I really think. I don't see the point of Kiev forcibly holding onto Luhansk and Donetsk – after all, they've been hindering the political development of the country all these years!

Navalny When I said something similar about Crimea, the whole of Ukrainian society just rounded on me. The annexation of Crimea was undoubtedly illegal. We violated the provisions of the Budapest Memorandum and the Russian-Ukrainian partnership agreement.[106] And in the long term this will only be detrimental for Russia. But we must understand that the problem of Crimea is of a political rather than legal character. And it cannot be solved purely by legal means. More than two million Russian passports have been issued to Crimea's residents, you can't cancel them just like that. So the only thing we can do is to annul the results of the farce of March 2014 and hold a fair and transparent referendum under international supervision. And accept the results, whatever they may be.

Michnik Ukrainian politicians are perfectly aware of the fact that the loss of Crimea has opened up new prospects for Ukraine.

Navalny But they don't say it out loud.

Michnik Of course not! That'd be suicide!

Navalny That's the astuteness of Putin's plan, right there. He's changed the domestic political agenda in Ukraine. Now every Ukrainian politician simply has to declare that Crimea will be returned. At the same time everyone understands the issue cannot be solved through the efforts of one side alone. Instead of building a democratic state, they're now going to be discussing what prospects there are for the return of Crimea.

No one's emerged a winner from the Crimea affair – everyone's lost out. Ukraine's now too preoccupied with this issue to discuss the truly important issues of internal development. Russia's been slapped with sanctions and can't develop normally either. And Crimea's turned into a "grey area" – nobody recognises it as part of Russia, which means that it, too, won't be developing properly.

Michnik I agree. Everyone's lost out. The Crimeans too.

Navalny Of course.

Michnik Solving this problem requires political will. And this can only come from Russia. All Ukrainian politicians can do now is repeat, "Crimea is ours!" over and over.

Navalny Absolutely right. Just like Greek politicians and Cyprus, the British and the Falklands, and the Japanese and the Northern Territories [the Kuril Islands]. Most Russian people have never laid eyes on the Kurils, but no Russian politician would ever say, "We don't need them, I'm giving them back to Japan."

Michnik Even Yeltsin was afraid to do that.

Navalny Of course he was. Foreign ministers can make eyes at each other and drop any number of hints, but no one's going to admit this publicly. So I'll say it honestly: the Crimea problem's going to be around for decades. It's impossible to resolve it in a way that'll satisfy every party. The best thing we can do is annul the result of the old referendum and hold a new one.

Michnik We need to ask the Crimeans what they want. And, of course, one of the most pivotal factors in the future of Crimea is going to be the status of the Crimean Tatars – the true "owners" of the peninsula and the victims of terrible Stalin-era repression.

Navalny I believe that, working in dialogue with the international community, we'll be able to develop a mechanism to ensure the representativeness and transparency of the referendum. That's the most important thing. And, of course, we need to ensure a level playing field for everyone involved and to provide a sufficient period of campaigning time (perhaps a year or six months). Those taking part in the referendum will need to be aware exactly what it is they're voting for.

Michnik There are international precedents for this – the referendum in the Saar region, for instance.[107]

Navalny Yes, we've researched that. We might recall the recent referendum in Scotland as well. There are examples of events of this kind being properly organised. And we can do the same, too.

Michnik What's your view of Strelkov, Zakharchenko and the rest?

Navalny They're very different people. Strelkov is someone who systematically adheres to his ideological positions. Despite the fact that they're completely alien to me, I'm forced to concede that he's a genuine proponent of Russian imperialist nationalism. He genuinely believes that there's no such thing as Ukraine, and that it's necessary to create (or recreate) some sort of Orthodox Soviet Union – complete with all its foreign colonies, and stretching from the German border to Vladivostok. He does perhaps recognise that Poles and Ukrainians aren't quite Russians as such, but he also believes that they're misguided children who need to be returned to the fold and taught how to live properly. And that America and Europe are common enemies we need to confront together. And all this is topped off by White-Guard-type paraphernalia: tsarist top-brass ideals, epaulets, whiskers, etc. In his eyes, Kiev is the "mother of Russian cities" and should be returned to Russia. He'd *perhaps* give Lvov to Poland, but Poland would be firmly in the Russian sphere of influence. I mean, what can you really say about all this? This is imperiality of the most hellish kind. Until very recently, people of this sort were marginalised even within nationalist circles – they were branded *imperasts* [supporters of empire or imperialist political projects]. And now it's a mainstream thing.

We have to understand that while Strelkov is genuinely striving to realise his imperialist project, the war with Ukraine is merely a *domestic* political manoeuvre from where Putin is standing. He's inciting militaristic hysteria for one purpose only – to remain in power and die peacefully in his bed as Tsar of Russia. Strelkov and his nationalist project represent a real threat. Zakharchenko and the like, on the other hand, are local crooks hired by the Kremlin to further its own interests. They're puppets.

Michnik Interesting. I think it's very important to realise that the conflict currently developing in Ukraine is a conflict of *values* – a clash of divergent ideas about what constitutes the "correct" world order. And the same thing is happening in Russia apropos Ukraine. Every event is being evaluated according to a value system.

Navalny I agree. That's why it's so crucial for Russia's democratic opposition that Ukraine manages to pull itself out of the crisis before establishing a democratic, European-style state.

12

Rewriting History

Navalny We've met on the eve of a massive anniversary – seventy years since the Victory over the Germans. And we can see that this, too, has been endowed with a special significance, becoming a factor in both domestic and foreign policy.

Michnik Victory Day has become a very multi-faceted phenomenon in the current situation. We know this is a special day for Russian society – a moment of utmost pride and honour. In spite of all the lies and barbarity surrounding this war, it was a war for a just cause. The Red Army soldiers were fighting not only for Stalin and Russia but for peace as well. But there are three important issues we mustn't lose sight of.

Firstly, the history of the war isn't black and white. Collaborationism took place, and it's important to understand the reasons for that. Secondly, it's important for this celebration to be a celebration for everybody. It's not for nothing that Solzhenitsyn, who fought in the Red Army but spent Victory Day in the Gulag, said that this victory was "not for us."[108] No doubt that was also the opinion of *Armia Krajowa* [Home Army] General Leopold Okulicki, arrested by the NKVD in 1945 and murdered in Moscow.[109] Thirdly, we must recognise the criminal nature of the Molotov-Ribbentrop Pact, the Soviet invasion of Poland on September 17, 1939, the annexation of the Baltic States and

Bessarabia, and Soviet collaboration with Hitler before the Great Patriotic War. Of course, Putin prefers to disremember such unpleasant things, and uses the celebration to legitimise his own power, implanting his own persona into a moment of utmost national honour. But that's the way it was in previous years, too. Now, though, he's introduced another layer of meaning into the event – it's come to serve as a legitimisation of his Ukraine policy. The implication is, we fought against fascism seventy years ago and prevailed, and now fascism is back and we'll prevail again – and this despite the fact that a conference of European fascists was held in St Petersburg weeks before the celebration and the authorities didn't regard this as a problem. And, of course, the rehabilitation of Stalinism is a very dangerous issue. It's time to openly admit that Stalin was a totalitarian executioner and tyrant. And not at all a "brilliant manager," as is now common practice to call him here.

Navalny I agree. We can remember the previous anniversaries of 1995 and 2005, when many veterans were still alive and the living memory of the war burned brighter than today. There were no problems then. And now they've suddenly materialised. Putin is simply taking terms every Russian can understand (fascists, punitive expeditioners,[110] Banderovites) and deploying them in a new political context. In this kind of situation, there can be absolutely no question of acquiring a new and clearer understanding of the dark pages of the war's history. But it's this we need to work towards.

A lot of archives have been opened in Russia recently, but by no means all of them. I think the main task of the state, its main duty to the war's victorious combatants, is to bury the remains of fallen soldiers and, if possible, to establish the names of the war's every participant. Entire regions of Russia are littered with the bones of Soviet soldiers. These people remain unidentified and unburied. How can we talk about any kind of remembrance until this is done? Other countries that were part of the anti-Hitler coalition have similar problems, too; in most of these, however, the deaths of soldiers with unknown fates are measured in the hundreds, while we have *hundreds of thousands*, if not millions! It's an insult to Russia. I think the most important war-related national project of all would involve ascertaining the exact number of victims, searching for their remains, identifying them, and committing them to the ground.

Michnik What's your view on the Ukrainian memorial laws that were passed in early April?[111]

Navalny In my opinion, this is a chief hallmark of bad politicians: having come to power, the first thing these people do is grab the history books and frantically proceed to rewrite them before issuing laws on the matter to boot. This isn't the way it should be. What they, as *politicians*, should be doing is opening the archives and encouraging the development of historical scholarship. So let them do just that. Everything else is for professional *historians* to debate. I understand why this is happening in Ukraine: the country is in a state of war, and the St George ribbon, which in Russia is a symbol of victory over fascism, has become a separatist symbol there. But that doesn't negate the fact that history is a subject for historians and not for politicians.

Michnik As a historian, I agree with you 100%, but as a politician – even as a former one – I can't quite concur. I'm very happy that Russian politicians have openly acknowledged that Katyn was Stalin's doing. And it's very important that this was done precisely by *politicians*. As a historian, I'm against criminal prosecution for Holocaust denial. But in certain situations, historical issues should be publicly subjected to a fundamental political assessment. Under normal circumstances, of course, politicians shouldn't be allowed to stray into the sphere of history.

Navalny There are established facts that cannot be denied, and politicians must, of course, acknowledge and articulate them. Especially if these facts poison relations among nations if they remain unacknowledged. Katyn is a case in point. But the problem is that, as a rule, politicians' meddling with historical matters creates more problems than it solves. There are different cultures of war remembrance in Ukraine, and this issue cannot be solved by legislative means. That's really my main point.

Michnik Russia's "historical" legislative initiatives have parallels in Poland. The national chauvinists, for example, argue that you can't write about Polish collaborationism. But what if it really did happen! That's not slander, is it! And then, of course, there's Polish anti-Semitism, which cannot be rooted out by legal means. It's the same thing with that proposed anti-Russophobia law in Russia. Is it really possible to ban people from being Russophobic? When Lermontov wrote "Farewell, unwashed Russia,"[112] was he being Russophobic? Nonsense!

Navalny We can recall all too well when the idea of a single history textbook was first seriously mooted – concurrently with the elimination of political and civil liberties. Imposing a history textbook on people is idiocy. It can result only in a distortion of history and in the impoverishment of our historical knowledge. There's never going to be complete agreement among historians, and the most wonderful thing you can imagine would be a series of high-profile historical symposia.

Let professionals come and discuss documents from public archives for weeks on end. Now that'd be great. In the end, of course, they'd all fall out and go their separate ways without arriving at any common point of view. But it'd still give us an opportunity to familiarise ourselves with all their opinions. And that'd be moving in the right direction.

There's a party in Russia that's even incorporated the agenda of de-Stalinisation into its political programme. That party is Yabloko. I think this is quite an artificial thing. How can you carry out de-Stalinisation by political means? Issue a load of prohibitive laws? I regard Stalin as the chief executioner of the Russian people – on the same level as Hitler. But I still don't understand what de-Stalinisation means in practice.

Michnik It means official recognition of Stalin's crimes.

Navalny But there's already official recognition of them.

Michnik But obstacles keep getting put in the way of people who expound on the crimes of Stalinism or try to erect monuments to its victims!

Navalny And that's totally unacceptable. But I think the real problem lies elsewhere. We don't need artificial de-Stalinisation and we don't need artificial re-Stalinisation. Greater familiarisation with the facts would be sufficient. Stalin's crimes are so flagrant, palpable and disgusting that the more we come to know about them, the quicker genuine de-Stalinisation will be realised. The Internet was recently awash with discussion of an interesting archival document – a secret dispatch to Stalin from People's Commissar of State Security Vsevolod Merkulov informing him on June 17, 1941 (five days before the war began!) that a source at the German Aviation Headquarters had confirmed that a

German invasion was imminent. Stalin scribbled across the document that this was no "source," this was a disinformant who should be told to "go fuck his mother." This is the sort of stuff that needs to be uncovered and published. Then everything will become clear.

The Russian journalist Sergei Parkhomenko is working on a wonderful project at the moment – it's called *Last Known Address*.[113]

Michnik Yes, I saw that. Great stuff!

Navalny It's a brilliant idea! And it doesn't require any help from the government, no bureaucratic nonsense. The important thing is not to interfere.

Michnik But if, say, the president were to play his part in the setting up of a memorial plaque, it would receive wider coverage and the effect would be amplified!

Navalny Of course. You can't do without gestures of this sort, without a doubt. But this isn't something you'd find in the programmes of political parties.

Michnik There's too much sentimentilisation of Stalin in Russian society, and a specific policy on this issue will probably be required. Charles de Gaulle did a lot to demonstrate that the real France was not the France of Pétain but the France of the Resistance. It's important to show that the real Russia is not a country whose love for Stalin is flourishing. I do agree that we don't need politicians to make forays into the domain of history, but, given that the images of Stalin and Hitler have become so deeply rooted in human memory, we have to do something about it.

Navalny We shouldn't artificially impose anything on people, that's all. We have to tread very delicately. Action always begets counteraction and, given how interventions of this ilk have generally been carried out in Russia, it's better for the state to steer clear of history in general. The main thing is to open all the archives and to encourage research in this area. The well-known Russian economist Sergei Guriev and his colleagues have produced a remarkable study into the effectiveness of Stalinist industrialisation, demonstrating that the horrific sacrifices of human lives could have been avoided.[114] It's been drilled into people's minds that Stalin was a super-effective manager who took Russia from the wooden plough to the atomic bomb. But research has shown that this isn't the case. Russia would've still graduated from the plough without any Stalin at the helm. Such conclusions should be drawn by experts before making their way into textbooks and into the minds of the people at large. The state can only support this process, not impose a single "correct" perspective on the past upon us.

My grandmother was in action throughout the whole war and even scrawled her name on the wall of the Reichstag. Her sister, meanwhile, was subjected to repression and exiled to Vorkuta. Grandma had read *The Gulag Archipelago* back in Soviet times (my mother recalls that we had this book at home) and agreed with everything written there. In her eyes, though, Stalin was "our everything" because he won the war for Russia.

Michnik If you crave greatness, then in your eyes Stalin may well be the leader in the war against Hitler. For many, this victory redeems everything else.

We have to open the archives – a lengthy process. It's a particularity of today's Russia that, in spite of all the lies spawned by Putinist propaganda, you can go into a Moscow bookshop, buy yourself a book and find out the whole truth about Stalin. It's now a matter for civil society. Gone are the days when Bukovsky quipped he'd believe in the "thaw" when making a photocopy became a mere triviality.

Fortunately for Putin, the Russian people don't read books. But we need to make them read – and good books, too. And this is a matter for civil society, not for the state.

Navalny Absolutely spot on! Parkhomenko has done a hundred times more for the cause of de-Stalinisation without a penny of public money behind him than any politician shouting "De-Stalinisation, de-Stalinisation, de-Stalinisation ..." a hundred times over from the speaker's stand.

Michnik Schoolchildren and students should be invited along to attend the unveilings of these memorial plaques. Then these events would have a political dimension of sorts.

Navalny This really is more of a task for civil society – a task for teachers and parents who believe in the necessity of it all. It's important we have more and more people like that. And we certainly will have more: re-Stalinisation and the new cult of personality are artificial processes orchestrated and funded by the state. I'm absolutely convinced that things will naturally develop in the direction of de-Stalinisation. Because no normal person reading core archival documents and memoirs would ever deny the fact of Stalin's repressions or the severity of his crimes.

If there is hope, it lies in the conscience of the people.

Michnik As it ever has done!

About the Interlocutors

Alexei Navalny (1976-) is a Russian public and political figure. Involved in public affairs since 2000, he was a member of the Yabloko party between 2000 and 2007, and co-founded the patriotic Narod [People] movement in 2008. The author of a popular anti-corruption blog, he helped mastermind the mass protests of 2011-2012. In 2010 he launched the *Rospil* ("Russian Kickbacks") anti-corruption project, setting in motion the work of the Anti-Corruption Foundation. He participated in the Moscow mayoral election of 2013, polling 27.2% of the vote. Navalny is the chairman of the unregistered Progress Party.

Adam Michnik (1946-) is a Polish human rights activist, journalist and public figure. He was an active participant in the mass student protests of 1968. In 1976-1977 he lived in exile in Paris. Upon returning to Poland, he joined the Workers' Defence Committee and managed a major underground publishing house. One of the key figures in the strike movement of August 1980, he also coordinated the trades union movement in the Masovian Voivodeship. After the introduction of martial law in December 1981, he was interned and spent three years in prison without sentence before being arrested once again in 1985, ultimately spending a total of more than six years in the prisons of the Polish People's Republic. One of Lech Wałęsa's closest advisers in 1988-1989, he took part in the Round Table Talks between the Communist government and the Solidarity-led opposition. In 1989 he was elected to the Sejm. Michnik is the founder and editor-in-chief of the daily social and political newspaper *Wyborcza*, which has been in circulation since 1990.

Daniel Treisman (Foreword)

Daniel Treisman is Professor of Political Science at the University of California, Los Angeles. He received his Ph.D. in Government from Harvard University in 1995. His work focuses on the politics and political economy of Russia, and on comparative political economy (in particular, the determinants of good government and the politics of macroeconomic policy). His latest book is *The Return: Russia's Journey from Gorbachev to Medvedev*, The Free Press, 2011.

Glossary

Akhmadulina, Bella (1937-2010): Soviet-Russian poetess.

Akhmatova, Anna (1889-1966): Russian poetess. Focusing her attention on the themes of time passing, and memory (of better times ...), her work was criticised and censored by the authorities, but she chose to remain in St Petersburg, her very presence a reminder of what Stalinism had done to the world she wrote about.

Alexander II (1818-1881): Emperor of Russia, 1855-1881.

Alexei II (1929-2008): Patriarch of Moscow and All-Russia, 1990-2008.

Alexeyeva, Lyudmila (1927-): Russian historian, Russian-Soviet human rights activist, founding member of the ground-breaking Moscow Helsinki Watch Group.

Amalrik, Andrei (1938-1980): Soviet writer and dissident. Author of the provocative essay, "Will the Soviet Union Survive Until 1984?"

Andropov, Yuri (1914-1984): Soviet politician. A complex man to evaluate: Soviet *apparatchik* who persuaded Khrushchev to put down by military force the 1956 Hun- garian Uprising; the man who as head of the KGB hounded Soviet dissidents; and yet who, as General Secretary of the Communist Party, from 12 November, 1982 until his death fifteen months later (succeeded first by Konstantin Chernenko, from 13 February, 1984 until he died thirteen months later, on 10 March, 1985; then by his protégé

Mikhail Gorbachev), instigated an anti-corruption campaign, which we can now see more clearly from a distance, was an acknowledgement of the failings of the socialist planned economy.

Andrzejewski, Jerzy (1909-1983): Polish writer, author of the novel *Ashes and Diamonds* (1948), one of the founders of the Committee for the Protection of Workers.

Aveyde, Oscar (1837-1897): Polish revolutionary, one of the leaders of the January Uprising of 1863-1864. Arrested in September 1863 and sent to Vyatka. His testimony given during questioning was later summarised in a separate volume for the emperor. Reprinted in 1961 as *Indications and Notes on the Polish Uprising of 1863*.

Balcerowicz, Leszek (1947-): Minister of Finance of Poland in 1989-1991 and 1997-2000; President of the National Bank, 2001-2007.

Bandera, Stepan (1909-1959): Head of the Organisation of Ukrainian Nationalists (Banderites). With the support of the Nazis, he planned to restore the sovereign Ukrainian state, but Hitler did not agree to his terms of cooperation. In 1941 sent to the Sachsenhausen camp, released in 1944, and went into exile.

Bartoszewski, Vladislav (1922-2015): Polish historian, Auschwitz prisoner, member of the Warsaw Uprising of 1944, professor of informal science courses in 1978-1981. After the "Velvet Revolution," Ambassador to Austria (1990-1995); Minister of Foreign Affairs of Poland in 1995 and 2000-2001.

Berezovsky, Boris (1946-2013): Russian oligarch, one of the key characters in the political arena of the 1990s. As one of the so-called "Seven bankers," contributed to the re-election of Boris Yeltsin as president in 1996.

Berlusconi, Silvio (1936-): Prime Minister of Italy in 1994-1995, 2001-2006, 2008-2011.

Bielecki, Yan Krzysztof (1951-): Leading figure of Solidarity; Prime Minister of Poland in 1991.

Brandt, Willy (1913-1992): West German Social Democrat, Minister of Foreign Affairs of the Federal Republic of Germany 1966-1969; Federal Chancellor 1969-1974. Nobel Peace Prize (1971).

Brecht, Bertolt (1898-1956): German poet, playwright, theatre director.

Brezhnev, Leonid (1906-1982): First (from 1966, General) Secretary of the CPSU Central Committee in 1964-1982.

Brodsky, Joseph (1940-1996): Russian-American poet and essayist. Nobel Prize for Literature (1987).

Brzezinski, Zbigniew (1928-): American political scientist and statesman of Polish origin. National Security Adviser to US President Jimmy Carter's administration 1977-1981.

Budyonny, Semyon (1883-1973): Commander of the First Cavalry Army (1919-1923) during Russian Civil War; Marshal of the Soviet Union (1935); Member of the Supreme Command 1941-1945; three times Hero of the Soviet Union.

Bukovsky, Vladimir (1942-): Soviet dissident and political émigré; author of the memoir *And the Wind Returns* (2007).

Bulgakov, Mikhail (1891-1940): Russian-Soviet writer, author of the novels *The White Guard* (1924) and *The Master and Margarita* (written 1929-1940, published 1966-1967).

Bush Jr, George (1946-): US President 2001-2009.

Buzek, Jerzy (1940-): Leading member of Solidarity; Prime Minister of Poland 1997-2001.

Ceausescu, Nicolae (1918-1989): Leader of Romania (1965-1989). The only communist leader to have been executed as a result of the Velvet Revolution.

Chaadaev, Pyotr (1794-1856): Russian philosopher and imperial dissident (before the word existed). Author of the eight "Philosophical Letters," written in French between 1826-31; they were banned in Russia, for their scathing criticism of the Romanov regime, but circulated in manuscript, and perhaps for that very reason, exerted a considerable influence on liberal Russians.

Chekhov, Anton (1860-1904): Russian writer of short stories and plays.

Chubais, Anatoly (1955-): Russian politician and state businessman. As head of the State Committee for the Management of State Property (1991-1994), headed the privatisation of state industries. Minister of Finance 1997, Vice-Prime Minister 1997-1998. Head of RAO UES energy company 1998-2008. Since 2008, head of Rosnano nanotechnology company.

Chukovsky, Kornei (1882-1969): Soviet-Russian writer and literary critic.

Cohn-Bendit, Daniel (1945-): French-German politician. Known as "Dany le rouge" (on account of his politics and his hair), he was a student leader during the disturbances of May 1968 in France. He was co-president of the European Greens-European Free Alliance in the European Parliament. Supporter of a federalist Europe.

Daniel, Yuli (1925-1988): Soviet writer and dissident.

Danton, Georges (1759-1794): Leading figure in the French Revolution. He was the first President of the Committee for Public Safety, but proved not to be revolutionary enough for some; and was guillotined.

Djilas, Milovan (1911-1995): Yugoslav politician, communist, organiser of the anti-fascist partisan movement in Yugoslavia, 1945-1954. For criticism of the party elite (the "new class"), removed from all leadership positions, and arrested; in prison for 7 years. From 1966, engaged in dissident activities. Author of The *New Class: An Analysis of the Communist System* (1957) and *Conversations with Stalin* (1961).

Dienstbier Jr., Jiri (1969-): Czech politician. Minister for Human Rights and Equal Opportunity in 2014.

Dostoevsky, Fyodor (1821-1881): Russian writer, author of the novels *Crime and Punishment* (1866), *The Possessed* (1872), *The Brothers Karamazov* (1880).

Dubček, Alexander (1921-1992): Slovak politician. First

Secretary of the Central Committee of the Communist Party of Czechoslovakia 1968-1969. Initiator of liberalisation in Czechoslovakia, known as the Prague Spring. Removed from his post after the Soviet invasion in 1968.

Dugin, Aleksandr (1962-): Russian philosopher whose ideas are said to be influential in the Kremlin under Vladimir Putin. Founder and leader of the International Eurasian Movement.

Eidelman, Natan (1930-1989): Soviet historian and writer, author of a popular academic book on the history of Russia in the 18th and 19th centuries.

Erenburg, Ilya (1891-1967): Soviet-Russian writer and publisher, author of the novel *Burya* (1947).

Fiszbach, Tadeusz (1935-): Polish statesman. First Secretary of the Gdansk Regional Committee of the Polish United Workers' Party in August 1980, maintained a loyal position towards the striking workers. Spoke out against the use of military force in 1981.

Francis, Pope, born Bergoglio, Jorge Mario (1936-): Bishop of Rome, Pope of the Roman Catholic Church since 2013.

Gaddafi, Muammar (1942-2011): Leader of the Libyan Republic, 1969-2011; killed during the civil war.

Gaidar, Yegor (1956-2009): Soviet-Russian liberal economist, acting Prime Minister in 1992.

Galich, Aleksandr (1918-1977): Soviet writer, poet, singer-songwriter, playwright, screenwriter, dissident and émigré.

Gandhi, Mahatma (1869-1948): Indian political figure, leader of the anti-colonial, non-violent movement in India.

Gaulle, Charles de (1890-1970): French military and political leader. Head of the French Resistance during the Second World War. Creator of the Fifth Republic (1958), and its first president (1959-1969).

Geremek, Bronislaw (1932-2008): Polish historian, leading member of Solidarity. Minister of Foreign Affairs, 1997-2000.

Giedroyc, Jerzy (1906-2000): Polish émigré, founder, publisher and longtime chief editor of "Culture" magazine, 1947-2000.

Gierek, Edward (1913-2001): Polish Communist politician. First Secretary of the Polish United Workers' Party, 1970-1980.

Glemp, József (1929-2013): Polish Cardinal of the Roman Catholic Church; Primate of Poland, 1981-2009.

Gogol, Nikolai (1809-1852): Russian writer, leading exponent of Realism, he satirised the Russian Empire in *The Government Inspector* (1836) and *Dead Souls* (1842).

Gomulka, Wladyslav (1905-1982): Polish Communist politican. First Secretary of the Polish United Workers' Party, 1956-1970.

González, Felipe Marquez (1942-): Spanish Social-Democrat politician. Prime Minister of Spain, 1982-1996.

Gorbachev, Mikhail (1931-): Soviet politician, identified with the reformist policies of *glasnost* (openness) and *perestroika* (restructuring). General Secretary of the Central Committee of the Communist Party in 1985-1991, when the party was dissolved. President of the USSR, 1990-1991.

Gorbanevskaya, Natalia (1936-2013): Soviet-Russian poetess and translator, dissident.

Grigorenko, Pyotr (1907-1987): Officer of the Red Army (Major General, 1959), veteran of the Second World War, dissident, émigré.

Grishin, Viktor (1914-1992): Soviet Communist politician. First Secretary of the Moscow City Party Committee, 1967-1985; member of the Politburo, 1971-1986.

Gross, Jan Tomasz (1947-): American historian and political scientist of Polish origin; Professor of History at Princeton University; author of *Neighbors: The Destruction of the Jewish Community in Jedwabne, Poland* (2000), and *Fear: Anti-Semitism in Poland after Auschwitz* (2006).

Guriev, Sergei (1971-): Russian economist. Rector of the New Economic School, 2003-2013, when he fled to France. Professor of economics at the Institut d'études politiques (Sciences Po) in Paris.

Gusinsky, Vladimir (1952-): Russian oligarch, founder of Media-Most holding company.

Gwiazda, Andrzej (1935-): Leading member of Polish Workers' Defence Committee, one of the organisers and leaders of the strike in Gdansk in August 1980, who took an active part in the creation of Solidarity. Subsequently, critic and political opponent of Lech Wałęsa, whom he considers an agent of the Communist secret services.

Havel, Václav (1936-2011): Czechoslovak writer and dissident. President of Czechoslovakia 1989-1992, then the Czech Republic, 1993-2003.

Herzen, Alexander (1812-1870): Russian writer and intellectual, often described as the "father of Russian socialism." In the 1850s and 1860s, in Russia, and later in exile in London, his political writings were enormously influential, at once excoriating the excesses of the Romanov regime, and setting out a liberal agenda, which achieved its apogee with the emancipation of the serfs in 1861.

Hitler, Adolf (1889-1945). German politician. Founder and Chairman of the National Socialist German Workers' (Nazi) Party (1921-1945). Chancellor of Germany, 1933-1945, Führer (leader) from 1934.

John Paul II, Pope (born Karol Józef Wojtyla, 1920-2005). Archbishop of Kraków, from 1964. Pope of the Roman Catholic Church, from 1978; his visit to Poland in 1979 contributed to the rise of Solidarity, and the demise of the Communist regime.

Jaruzelski, Wojciech (1923-2014): Polish military leader and statesman. Minister of Defence (1968-1983); Prime Minister (1981-1985); First Secretary of the Central Committee of the Polish United Workers' Party (1981-1989). Imposed martial law in December 1981, subsequently oversaw the peaceful transition from Communism to an opposition-led government (1989).

Kaczynski, Jaroslaw (1949-): Polish conservative politician and lawyer. Member of Solidarity in the 1980s, executive editor of *Tygodnik Solidarnosć* newspaper. Founded 1991, Christian Democrat Centre Agreement party, chairman until 1998. Prime Minister of Poland, 2006-2007. Co-founder, and leader of the right-wing Law and Justice party since 2010.

Kaczynski, Lech (1949-2010): Polish conservative politician. Activist in pro-democracy, anti-Communist movement 1970s; member of Solidarity in the 1980s; co-founder (2001) of the right-wing Law and Justice party (2001). President of Poland, 2005-2010. He died in a plane crash near Smolensk on April 10, 2010.

Kadyrov, Ramzan (1976-): Head of the Chechen Republic of the Russian Federation, from 2007.

Kalugin, Oleg (1934-): Member of the Soviet KGB, rank of major general. After retirement (1989) publicly criticised and denounced the work of the Communist security forces; published T*he First Directorate: My 32 Years in Intelligence and Espionage Against the West* (1994). In 1995 emigrated to the United States. In 2002, convicted in absentia for treason and sentenced to 15 years in prison.

Kasyanov, Mikhail (1957-): Russian liberal politician. Prime Minister, 2000-2004. Co-chairman of the opposition "People's Freedom Party" since 2012.

Khodorkovsky, Mikhail (1963-): Russian businessman, former head of the oil company Yukos, founder of the Open Russia movement. One of the men known as the "oligarchs," who accumulated wealth and power during the 1990s. A vocal, public opponent of Vladimir Putin, he was arrested in 2003 in connection with an alleged fraud, and spent ten years in prison. He was pardoned in 2013, and has become a political émigré promoting the vision of an alternative (liberal democratic) Russia.

Khrushchev, Nikita (1894-1971): First Secretary of the Central Committee of the Communist Party of the Soviet Union (1953-1964); Chairman of the Council of Ministers of the USSR (1958-1964). Responsible for the de-Stalinisation of the Soviet Union, he initiated a policy of cautious domestic liberalisation, and was in power at the height of the Cold War, a period marked by a number of crises, including the downing of the American U-2 spy plane, and the Cuban Missile Crisis.

Kirill I, Patriarch, born Vladimir Mikhailovich Gundyayev (1946-): Patriarch of Moscow and All Russia, Primate of the Russian Orthodox Church since 2009. A doctrinal conservative, and Putin supporter, has described people demonstrating for democratic reform and the rule of law as giving out "ear piercing shrieks." His private and financial life has attracted media attention for the apparent inconsistencies with a religious vocation.

Kiszczak, Czeslaw (1925-): Polish Communist politician. Minister of Internal Affairs, 1981-1990. The last Communist Prime Minister of Poland, serving for seventeen days in August 1989.

Kolakowski, Leszek (1927-2009): Polish political philosopher and historian of ideas. Best known for his analyses of Marxist thought, particularly in *Main Currents of Marxism* (1976).

Komarovskaya, Maya (1937-): Polish actress and opposition activist; during martial law, refused to appear on television, and assisted the detained leaders of Solidarity. Her films include a number of Polish classics: *A Year of the Quiet Sun,* directed by Krzysztof Zanussi (1984); *The Maids of Wilko* (1979); *Man of Iron* (1981); *Katyn* (2007), all directed by Andrzej Wajda; *The Decalogue,* directed by Krzysztof Kieślowski (1988).

Komorowski, Bronislaw (1952-): Polish politician and historian. Activist in anti-Communist movement, worked on the underground publication *Glos*. Member of the centrist Civic Platform party in 2001. President of Poland, 2010-2015.

Korwin-Mikke, Janusz (1942-): Polish politician and writer. Creator of the Polish libertarian and Eurosceptic political party, Coalition for the Renewal of the Republic - Liberty and Hope. Member of European Parliament.

Kouchner, Bernard (1939): French politician and physician. Co-founder of Médecins Sans Frontières and Médecins du Monde. Has been a minister in both left- and right-wing governments.

Kovalyov, Sergei (1930-): Soviet-Russian human rights activist and politician. Co-authored 1991 "Declaration of Human and Civil Rights in Russia," contributed to the drafting of Article 2 (Rights and Liberties of Man and Citizen) of Russian Constitution. People's Deputy of the Russian Federation (1990-1993); member of the Presidium of the Supreme Council of the Russian Federation; chairman of President's Human Rights Commission, and Human Rights Commissioner for the State Duma (member 1993-2003); member of the Russian delegation to the

Parliamentary Assembly of the Council of Europe. Having been an outspoken critic of the Soviet regime, he became an increasingly vocal critic of first Yeltsin's and then Putin's authoritarian tendencies.

Kozlowski, Krzysztof (1931-2013): Polish Communist politician. Minister of Internal Affairs, 1990-1991.

Kuchma, Leonid (1938-): Ukrainian politician. Member of the Central Committee of the Communist Party of Ukraine, but by end 1980s was a critic of Communism. Second President of independent Ukraine 1994-2005, his presidency notable for its corruption scandals and a failure to effect economic reforms.

Kundera, Milan (1929-): Czechoslovak (Czech) writer. Author of the novels *The Joke* (1967), *The Book of Laughter and Forgetting* (1979), *The Unbearable Lightness of Being* (1984). Since 1975, living in France, whose citizenship he adopted in 1981, soon after he was stripped of his Czechoslovak citizenship (1979).

Kuraev, Andrei (1963-): Orthodox theologian, writer. Proto-deacon of the Russian Orthodox Church. His published writing (*Harry Potter* is a favourite subject) has caused much debate in Russian society, particularly when talking about ethnicity, including "How to Relate to Islam after Beslan" (2004).

Kuroń, Jacek (1934-2004): Intellectual, and a leading theoretician of the democratic opposition in the Communist People's Republic of Poland, known as "the godfather of the Polish opposition." One of the founders of the Committee for the Protection of Workers (1976), and of

Solidarity (1980). Minister of Labour and Social Policy in 1989-1990, and in 1992-1993.

Kwaśniewski, Aleksandr (1954-): Polish politician and journalist. Communist student activist, 1970s. Minister of Youth Affairs, 1985-1987, under Communist government. Chairman of the Committee on Youth, Sports and Physical Education, 1987-1990. In post-communist Poland, he was a leader of the party Social Democracy of the Republic of Poland, and a co-founder of the Democratic Left Alliance. Defeated Lech Walesa for the presidency in 1995; re-elected 2000, to 2005.

Lavrov, Sergei (1950-): Russian diplomat. Foreign Minister since 2004. In public, loyal to the hard-line policy of the Kremlin, but not a policy that he has created.

Lenin, Vladimir, born Vladimir Ilyich Ulyanov (1870-1924): Revolutionary, and activist opposing the tsarist regime. Leader of the Bolshevik faction of the Russian Social-Democratic Labour Party (since 1903). Took a belated part in the failed revolution of February 1917 (he was in Zurich at the time), and played a leading role in the successful revolution of October 1917. Chairman of the Council of People's Commissars, 1917-1924.

Levada, Yuri (1930-2006): Soviet-Russian sociologist and political scientist. Founded with colleagues in 1988 the Russian Public Opinion Research Center (VCIOM). Founder and first director (2003-2006) of the Levada Centre, a non-governmental, analytical and polling organisation.

Le Pen, Marine (1968-): French politician. Since 2011 the

leader of the right-wing National Front party, founded by her father Jean-Marie Le Pen.

Lermontov, Mikhail (1814-1841): Russian Romantic writer of prose and poetry, "the poet of the Caucasus," best known as the author of the novel *A Hero of Our Time* (1840).

Limonov, Eduard (1943-): Soviet-Russian writer, émigré. Returned to Russia beginning of the 1990s, since taking an active part in political life. Creator of the National Bolshevik Party (1993), banned in 2007 as an extremist organisation. In 2003, sentenced to 4 years in prison for illegal possession of weapons (freed on parole).

Lukashenko, Aleksandr (1954-): Belarussian politician. President (since 1994) of an authoritarian regime.

Maksimov, Vladimir (1930-1995): Soviet-Russian writer. In 1974 emigrated to France, where he created the "Continent" magazine, whose chief editor he was until 1992.

Mandelstam, Osip (1891-1938): Russian poet, essayist, literary critic. During Stalinist purges of 1930s, sent into internal exile. Arrested again 1938. He died in a prison camp in 1938.

Mao Zedong (1893-1976): Chinese politician and statesman. One of the founders of the Chinese Communist Party. Chairman of the CPC Central Committee (1943-1976), and head of China (1949-1976).

Masaryk, Tomáš (1850-1937): Czech scientist, politician and statesman. First president of independent Czechoslovakia (1918-1935).

Mazowiecki, Tadeusz (1927-2013): Polish public and political figure. The first non-communist Prime Minister (1989-1991) in the modern history of the country.

Men, Aleksandr (1935-1990): Orthodox theologian and writer. Proto-deacon of the Russian Orthodox Church. A dissident whose writings were banned, he held an ecumenical position, set out in his *In Search of the Way, the Truth, and the Life* (volumes 1-6, Brussels, 1970-1983; 2nd edition, Moscow, 1991-1992).

Meroshevsky, Juliusz (1906-1976): Polish writer and journalist, émigré. Employed by, and a regular contributor to the magazine "Culture."

Michalik, Józef (1941-): Polish Roman Catholic bishop. Bishop of the Zielona Góra-Gorzów diocese, 1986-1993. Archbishop of Przemyśl in 1993. President of the Polish Episcopal Conference, 2004-2014.

Mickiewicz, Adam (1798-1855): Polish writer and political activist, often referred to as "the national poet." Romantic author of the poem *Konrad Wallenrod* (1828), *Pan Tadeusz* (1834), and the poetic drama *Dzyady* (*Forefathers' Eve*).

Mikhalkov, Nikita (1945-): Soviet-Russian film director. Three times nominated for an Oscar in the category of best foreign language film, won with *Burnt by the Sun* (1995). Also known for his nationalist views, and support of Vladimir Putin.

Milevskiy, Miroslav (1928-2008): Polish politician. Minister of Internal Affairs, 1980-1981. Curator of the law enforcement agencies in the party's Political Bureau, 1981-

1985. Dismissed shortly after the murder of Jerzy Popieluszko.

Milosz, Czeslaw, (1911-2004): Polish writer, émigré. Cultural attaché in Paris, and Washington, defected 1951. Author of *The Issa Valley* (1955), *In Search of A Homeland* (1992), and (non-fiction) *The Captive Mind* (1953), one of the key anti-Stalinism texts. Nobel Prize for Literature (1980).

Miodovich, Alfred (1929-): Polish trades union and political activist. Member of the Communist party's Political Bureau in 1986-1990, where he supervised the activities of the All-Poland Alliance of Trades Unions. Took part in the Polish Round Table Agreement.

Moczar, Mieczyslaw (1913-1986): Polish Communist politician. Minister of Internal Affairs, 1964-1968, leader of the "partisan" faction in the Polish United Workers' Party.

Modzelevsky, Karol (1937-): Polish historian and political activist. Expelled from Communist Polish United Workers Party for opposition activities. With Jacek Kuroń he co-wrote the "Open Letter to the Party," for which he was imprisoned for three years. Took part in the Polish 1968 political crisis, and was imprisoned for three and a half years. One of the founders of the Committee for the Protection of Workers, and Solidarity (he came up with the name). Left-wing member of Senate, 1989-1991.

Mubarak, Hosni (1928-): Egyptian politician. President, 1981-2011, ousted from power in a 2011 revolution, after which he became a defendant in several criminal cases, convicted in some.

Nekrasov, Viktor (1911-1987): Russian writer, émigré; author of the novel *Front-Line Stalingrad* (1946).

Nemtsov, Boris (1959-2015): Russian politician; Governor of Nizhny Novgorod region (1991-1997); Deputy Prime Minister (1997-1998); Co-chairman of the opposition "People's Freedom Party" (2012-2015). Murdered in Moscow, February 27, 2015.

Okudzhava, Bulat (1924-1997): Soviet-Russian poet, singer-songwriter, writer, scriptwriter, composer.

Okulitsky, Leopold (1989-1946): Lieutenant Colonel (last) of the Polish Home Army (1944-1945). Arrested by the NKVD in the spring of 1945; died in Lubyanka prison.

Orbán, Viktor (1963-): Hungarian politician; co-founder of the Fidesz party (1988); Prime Minister of Hungary (1998-2002) and again in 2010.

Orwell, George (1903-1950): English writer and author of the dystopian novel *1984* (1949).

Parkhomenko, Sergei (1964-): Russian journalist and editor of the newspaper *Itogi* 1996-2001; member of the Russian PEN International Centre for Writers since 2014; co-founder of several community projects ("Society of the Blue Buckets," "Dissernet," "Last Address").

Pavlova-Silvanskaya, Marina (1936-): Soviet-Russian historian and political scientist.

Pétain, Henri Philippe Benoni Omer Joseph (1856-1951): French military leader and statesman; hero of the Battle of

Verdun (1916); Marshal of France (1918); head of the collaborationist Vichy regime 1940-1944. In 1945 sentenced to death for treason; the sentence commuted to life imprisonment.

Petrov, Nikita (1957-): Russian historian; member of "Memorial" human rights centre.

Pilsudski, Józef (1867-1935): Polish military leader and statesman; first leader of the new Polish state (1918-1922); de facto dictator 1926-1935.

Pipes, Richard (1923-): Polish-American historian; author of *Russia under the Old Regime* (1974), *The Russian Revolution* (1990), *Property and Freedom* (1999).

Podrabinek, Aleksandr (1953-): Soviet dissident, political prisoner; one of the founders of the Working Commission for the Investigation of the Use of Psychiatry for Political Purposes, during the Moscow-Helsinki group (1977). Author of the memoir *Dissidents* (2014).

Popieluszko, Jerzy (1947-1984): Catholic priest, and supporter of Solidarity. Killed by members of the Security Services.

Poroshenko, Petro (1965-): Ukrainian businessman and politician; President of Ukraine since 2014.

Prokhanov, Aleksandr (1938-): Soviet-Russian writer and publisher, founder and lifelong editor-in-chief of the populist left-wing magazine "Zavtra" (founded 1993).

Przymanowski, Janusz (1922-1998): Polish writer, author of the novel *Four Tank-Men and a Dog* (1964); scriptwriter of the eponymous TV series (1966-1970).

Pugachev, Yemelyan (circa 1742-1775): Don Cossack, leader of the Cossack peasant uprising (1773-1775), the largest popular uprising in the history of pre-revolutionary Russia.

Pushkin, Aleksandr (1799-1837): Russian writer, author of the novel in verse *Eugene Onegin* (1823-1832), the poem *Ruslan and Lyudmila* (1817-1820), *The Fountain of Bakhchisarai* (1821-1823), *The Bronze Horseman* (1833), and the tragedy *Boris Godunov* (1825).

Putin, Vladimir (1953-): Lieutenant colonel of the Soviet KGB (1975-1991). Head of the FSB (1998-1999). Prime Minister of the Russian Federation (1999, 2008-2012). President (2000-2008 and again since 2012).

Rákosi, Mátyás (1892-1971): Revolutionary and Communist dictator of Hungary (1947-1956).

Rakowski, Mieczyslaw (1926-2008): Prime Minister of Poland (1988-1989); last appointed First Secretary of the Central Committee of the Polish United Workers' Party (1989-1990).

Reykowski, Janusz (1929-): Polish academic, professor of psychology, and politician. Member of the Polish United Workers' Party (1949-1990). On the eve of the talks with the opposition, he intervened in the Politburo as a representative of the liberal movement within the party. Participated in the work of the Round Table (1989).

Röhm, Ernst (1887-1934): German Nazi, leader of the Nazi Party militia, the SA (1931-1934). He was killed during the "Night of the Long Knives" (June 20, 1934) on the orders of Adolf Hitler.

Rogozin, Dmitri (1963-): Russian politician, founder of the pro-government nationalist party "Rodina;" Vice-Prime Minister from 2011.

Rosati, Dariusz (1946-): Polish economist and politician. Member of the Polish United Workers' Party (1966-1990). Polish Minister for Foreign Affairs (1995-1997).

Sachs, Jeffrey (1954-): American economist, professor at Harvard (1983-2002), and Columbia University (since 2002).

Sakharov, Andrei (1921-1989): Soviet academic and dissident; developer of the hydrogen bomb; co-founder of the Committee on Human Rights in the USSR (1970). Awarded the Nobel Peace Prize (1975). In 1980, sent to the closed city of Gorky (Nizhny Novgorod), freed in 1986. People's Deputy of the USSR, 1989.

Sheinis, Viktor (1931-): Russian-Soviet writer and economist, political thinker, co-founder of the left-wing liberal party "Yabloko."

Shenderovich, Viktor (1958-): Russian writer, scriptwriter, satirist. Best known for penning *Kukly* [Puppets], the TV show, which from 1994-2002 lampooned the political system. Has since become a vocal critic of the Putin regime.

Shevtsova, Lilia (1949-): Russian (born Ukrainian SSR) public intellectual. Senior Associate at Carnegie Endowment for International Peace.

Sikorski, Radoslaw (1963-): Polish Minister of Defence (2005-2007); Minister of Foreign Affairs (2007 - 2014).

Sinyavsky, Andrei (1927-1997): Soviet writer, dissident and émigré.

Solzhenitsyn, Aleksandr (1918-2008): Soviet-Russian writer, political prisoner, dissident, émigré. Author of *One Day in the Life of Ivan Denisovich* (1962), *The Gulag Archipelago* (1973), *The Red Wheel* (1983).

Stalin, Iosif (1879-1953): Secretary General of the Central Committee of various Soviet institutions, including the Communist Party of the Soviet Union (1922-1953); de facto dictator of the Soviet Union (1929-1953).

Stravinsky, Igor (1882-1971): Russian composer of operas, ballets, concertos, symphonies and chamber music; émigré.

Strelkov, Igor (1970-): pseudonym for Igor Girkin, a Russian former military officer, who took part in the fighting in Eastern Ukraine in 2014. Military commander of the forces of the self-proclaimed Donetsk People's Republic (May-August 2014).

Surkov, Vladislav (1964-): Russian businessman, politician, ideologue. First Deputy Chief of Presidential Administration (1999-2011), during which time he developed the ideology of sovereign democracy. A close adviser to Vladimir Putin. In a previous life, was head of advertising for Mikhail Khodorkovsky's Bank Menatep (1991-1996).

Suslov, Mikhail (1902-1982): Soviet politician, ideologue. Second Secretary of the Communist Party, from 1965. More than anyone in the Kremlin, responsible for a hardline anti-reformist ideology.

Szlajfer, Henryk (1947-): Polish economist, political thinker and diplomat. Participated in the student protests of 1968 and, together with Adam Michnik, excluded from Warsaw University, and then arrested.

Tchaikovsky, Pyotr (1840-1893): Russian Romantic composer of operas, ballets, concertos, symphonies and chamber music.

Tito, Iosip Broz (1892-1980): Yugoslav revolutionary, organiser of the anti-fascist partisan movement; leader of Yugoslavia (1945-1980).

Tolstoy, Lev (1828-1910): Russian writer, best known as the author of *War and Peace* (1865-1869), *Anna Karenina* (1875-1877).

Tsipko, Aleksandr (1941-): Soviet-Russian political scientist; assistant to Aleksandr Yakovlev, member of the Politburo of the Central Committee of the Communist Party of the Soviet Union (1988-1990).

Tukhachevsky, Mikhail (1893-1937): Soviet military leader and theoretician. Headed various divisions of the Red Army during the Russian Civil War, and the Soviet-Polish war of 1920. Deputy People's Commissar of Defence (1934-1937), then Marshal of the Soviet Union (1935). Accused of treason, executed in 1937, rehabilitated in 1957.

Turgenev, Ivan (1818-1883): Russian writer, author of *A Sportsman's Sketches* (collection of short stories, 1852), *MuMu* (short story, 1852), *Fathers and Sons* (novel, 1862), *Night* (1877).

Tusk, Donald (1957-): Polish politician and historian.

Activist member of Solidarity; Prime Minister of Poland (2007-2014); President of the European Council since 2014.

Verblan, Andrzej (1924-): Editor-in-Chief of the magazine *New Way* (organ of the Communist Party); member of the Politburo of the PUWP 1980-1981. Removed from his post for supporting the democratic reforms initiated by Solidarity.

Vysotsky, Vladimir (1938-1980): Soviet singer-songwriter, poet. His anti-establishment lyrics, and independent spirit gave him iconic status, which has endured to this day.

Wajda, Andrzej (1926-): Polish director whose works have paid much attention to Poland during the Second World War *(Ashes and Diamonds,* 1958; *The Crowned-Eagle Ring,* 1992; *Katyn,* 2007), and the activities of the opposition *(Man of Iron,* 1981; *Walesa: Man of Hope,* 2012). Four of his films have been nominated for the Academy Award for Best Foreign Language Film (1976, 1980, 1982, 2008). In 2000, awarded honorary Oscar.

Wałęsa, Lech (1943-): Leader of Solidarity; President of Poland 1990-1995.

Wyszyński, Stefan (1901-1981): Cardinal of the Roman Catholic Church. Primate of Poland 1948-1981.

Yakovlev, Aleksandr (1923-2005): Soviet party activist, Secretary of the Central Committee of the Communist Party of the Soviet Union for Ideological Matters (1986-1990), member of the Politburo (1987-1990). Known as the "Godfather of Glasnost," he is acknowledged as the man who gave an ideological underpinning to Gorbachev's reforms. In later life, as head of the Presidential Committee for the Rehabilitation of Victims of Political Repression, he worked tirelessly to publicise the victims of Soviet purges.

Yatsenyuk, Arseny (1974-): Ukrainian politician, economist and lawyer. Ukrainian Minister of the Economy (2005-2006), Minister of Foreign Affairs (2007), Prime Minister since 2014. Asked to resign by President Poroshenko, February 2016, but Ukrainian parliament declined to call a vote of confidence.

Yavlinsky, Grigory (1952-): Russian (born Ukraine) economist and politician. Author of the "500 Days Programme," the 1990 blueprint for the transformation of a Soviet planned economy into a free-market, in only two years. Leader of the liberal Yabloko party.

Yeltsin, Boris (1931-2007). Soviet-Russian politican. Member of the Politburo, resigned 1987. First elected President of Russia, 1991-1999.

Yew, Lee Kuan (1923-2015): Singapore politician and statesman. Prime Minister, 1959-1990, Senior Minister until 2004, then Minister Mentor. Creator of modern Singapore and the author of the local "economic miracle."

Yushchenko, Viktor (1954-): Prime Minister of Ukraine (1999-2001), President (2005-2010).

Zakharchenko, Alexander (1976-): Prime Minister of the self-proclaimed Donetsk People's Republic, since November 2014.

Zhirinovsky, Vladimir (1946-): Russian politician, founder and chairman of the Liberal Democratic Party of Russia (LDPR); deputy of the State Duma of the I-VI convocations.

Zubov, Andrey (1952-): Russian historian and political scientist. Dismissed from his position of Professor of the Moscow State Institute of International Relations, for criticising Putin's military intervention in Ukraine.

Zyuganov, Gennady (1944-): Russian politician. Chairman of the Communist Party of the Russian Federation (CPRF) since 1993; member of the State Duma of the I-VI convocations.

Endnotes

1 The Thaw of 1956, also known as Polish October, October 1956, Polish thaw, or Gomulka's thaw, describes the moment when Poland experienced some liberalisation, a transition that affected not only its relationship with Moscow, but Moscow's relationships with other satellite states. A combination of the reforming tendencies of Nikita Khrushchev in the Kremlin, and disturbances in June by workers in Poznań, directly led to the rise of Wladyslav Gomulka, head of a reformist group. Faced with concern in Moscow, which could have led to his dismissal, Gomulka stood his ground, giving Poland much greater autonomy. Although the thaw marked the end of Stalinisation, it was a false dawn for liberals, as Gomulka began to exercise an increasingly oppressive control.

2 Khrushchev's secret report, entitled *On the Personality Cult and its Consequences*, was read out at the Twentieth Congress of the CPSU in February 1956 and quickly found its way into Poland, where it was widely circulated (probably by mistake). That summer, the country experienced a wave of protests, of which the most intense took place in Poznan. Khrushchev, however, stopped short of sending troops into Poland, and, for the first time in an Eastern bloc country, the party leadership was overhauled without the direct approval of Moscow.

3   The Katyn massacre refers to the mass executions of Polish officers and intelligentsia, by the People's Commissariat for Internal Affairs (NKVD – secret police) in April and May 1940. It was Lavrenty Beria, head of the NKVD, who made the initial proposal to Moscow, to execute all the members of the Polish Officer Corps captured during the 1939 Soviet invasion of Poland. Stalin gave his approval, with the result that some 22,000 people were executed (in the Katyn forest in Russia, and in the Kalinin and Kharkiv prisons) not only some 8,000 Polish officers, but also 6,000 Polish police, and 8,000 Polish intellectuals.

4   The Molotov-Ribbentrop Pact was a non-aggression treaty signed in Moscow on 23 August 1939 by Soviet foreign minister Vyacheslav Molotov and German foreign minister Joachim von Ribbentrop, whereby Nazi Germany and the Soviet Union agreed not to go to war with each other, or interfere with the other's spheres of influence. The pact still exercises historians and politicians – both Sergei Lavrov and Vladimir Putin have spoken of it favourably.

5   The Prague Spring was the short-lived period (from 5 January 1968 to 21 August) of liberalisation in Communist Czechoslovakia. Having been elected First Secretary at the very beginning of 1968, the reformist Alexander Dubček attempted a partial decentralisation of the economy, with a loosening of restrictions on the media, free speech and foreign travel. Dubček also divided the country administratively into the Czech Republic and Slovak Republic, the only reforms that survived the August invasion by the Soviet Union and other Warsaw pact member countries, which put a halt to the liberalisation process.

6 Michnik's "national chauvinists" refers to the Mieczyslaw Moczar-led "Partisan Faction," which developed within the Polish United Workers' Party soon after the latter's appointment as Minister of Internal Affairs (1964). Ideologically, the group advocated a brand of National Stalinism, which entailed total control over the population and ridding the Communist Party of the influence of Jewish Communists.

7 The Six Day War in 1967 provided the "Partisans" (see note above) with a pretext to unleash an anti-Semitic campaign. They also regarded the student demonstrations of March 1968 as Zionist-inspired, and believed that their ultimate aim was to undermine the stability of the People's Republic.

8 As part of his *Ostpolitik* (or "New Eastern Policy", whose purpose was to normalise relations between the Federal Republic of Germany and the Eastern Bloc), Willy Brandt, the FRG's Social Democratic Chancellor, signed a series of agreements with the USSR and Poland in 1970, recognising the Oder-Neisse line as the Germany-Poland border.

9 The trial of writers Andrei Sinyavsky and Yuri Daniel (1965-1966) is one of the key events in the history of the dissident movement in the Soviet Union. Having no opportunity to publish in their native country, Sinyavsky and Daniel sent their work for publication in the West under the respective pseudonyms Abram Tertz and Nikolai Arzhak. When their identities were finally discovered, Sinyavsky and Daniel were charged under Article 70 of the RSFSR Criminal Code, and sentenced to seven and five years in prison, respectively.

A group of Moscow-based writers subsequently penned an open letter to the Presidium of the Twenty-Third Congress of the CPSU. "While we do not approve of the means resorted to by these writers in publishing their works abroad, we cannot accept the fact that their actions betray any anti-Soviet intent, evidence of which would be required for such a grave punishment to be meted out. No such malicious intent has been proven over the course of the Sinyavsky-Daniel trial."

10   Radio Free Europe was founded in 1949 by the US National Committee for a Free Europe – a non-governmental organisation funded by the CIA. The radio station's mission was (and remains) "to promote democratic values and institutions by reporting the news in countries where a free press is banned by the government or not fully established." In 1973, RFE merged with Radio Liberty (RL).

11   The Flying University (Uniwersytet Latający) and the Society of Scientific Courses (Towarzystwo Kursów Naukowych) were established as underground educational institutions in 1977 and 1978, respectively. Their prototypes were homonymous institutions operating on Polish territory in the late nineteenth and early twentieth centuries: the first Flying University was inaugurated in 1885 and was able to start operating legally some twenty years later, metamorphosing into the Society of Scientific courses in 1906. In the People's Republic, both institutions were destroyed in December 1981 following the introduction of martial law.

12 During the 1980 Moscow Olympic Games, the city was prettified and presented like a film set; everything choreographed perfectly for the eyes of the West.

13 With the direct support of Moscow, the Polish Communists took control of the country by falsifying the results of the parliamentary elections held on 19 January 1947. Officially, the Democratic Bloc, controlled by the communist Polish Workers Party (PPR), but also including the Polish Socialist Party (PPS), People's Party (SL), and Democratic Party, won 80.1% of the vote, and 394 of the 444 seats in the Sejm. The opposition Polish People's Party received 28 seats.

In practice, the victory had been stolen, by means of intimidation, outright violence, and voting fraud. In actuality the Democratic Bloc had won perhaps no more than 50% of the vote. But the "victory" was enough for the Communists to claim that they represented the voice of the people, and they set about consolidating their power.

In fear of their lives, and feeling betrayed by the lukewarm protests of Western governments, many members of opposition parties left the country.

Soon, there was no more talk of a coalition, and in 1948 the rump of the PPS was forced to merge with the Communists, to form the Polish United Workers Party.

14 A reference to the protests that broke out in 1970 in the northern Baltic coastal cities of Gdansk, Gdynia, Elblag and Szczecin. The immediate cause was the government raising without warning the prices of foodstuffs and other basic items. But there was another element to the conflagration – an increasing intolerance by the

Polish public of authoritarianism. Although the revolt was ruthlessly put down, with some 40 killed (the numbers are uncertain) and more than 1,000 wounded, the Gomulka government was brought down (as much by Moscow as anything else), Edward Gierek installed as leader, and economic and political reforms promised.

15 The Soviet-Polish war of 1919-21 grew out of a conflict between two emerging states: Poland, reborn in the wake of the First World War, and Soviet Russia, which came into being following the collapse of the Russian Empire and the October Revolution. In 1919, Lenin's government, preoccupied with the civil war, proposed settling the conflict by peaceful means, and went as far as to offer major territorial concessions to Poland. But the Józef Pilsudski-led Polish government justifiably feared Soviet expansion in the immediate aftermath of the internal Russian conflict. In the spring of 1920, after the defeat of A.I. Denikin's anti-Bolshevik armed forces of South Russia, and the occupation by the Red Army of the whole of left-bank and part of right-bank Ukraine, Pilsudski forged an alliance with the Ukrainian nationalist Simon Petliura, and marched his forces towards Kiev. The slow-burning Soviet-Polish conflict acquired a new dimension. In the initial stages of the war (April-May), Polish and Ukrainian forces enjoyed a degree of success and managed to seize Kiev. In June, however, the Red Army launched counter-offensives on the south-western and western fronts and initiated offensives on Warsaw and Lvov in the following two months. The assault on Warsaw proved unsuccessful: Pilsudski managed to regroup and counter-attack, inflicting a heavy defeat on the Red Army. The attempt to take Lvov also ended in failure. These setbacks

heralded a new phase in the war: in September-October 1920, Polish forces took Grodno and Minsk. Russia and her allies (the Belorussian and Ukrainian Soviet Socialist Republics) initiated peace talks with the Poles; an armistice was concluded on October 12, 1920, and the so-called Peace of Riga was signed on March 18 of the following year, with Western Ukraine and Western Belorussia being ceded to Poland.

16   "Socialism with a human face" was the reformist programme instituted by Alexander Dubček, and formalised at the Presidium of the Communist Party of Czechoslovakia in April 1968, only a few months after Dubček had become leader. It was a policy of reducing authoritarianism, but in no way a disavowal of communism. Even that small measure of reform, however, was too much for Moscow, which preferred its politics to be faceless and pliable. Only a few months later, that hopeful period, known as the Prague Spring, was brutally suppressed by Soviet and Warsaw Pact military forces.

17   Even before the loss of Polish statehood, the Catholic Church was an institution that served to bind the nation together. Despite the official atheism of the Communist regime, the Church retained its unique position in the People's Republic.

18   Karol Wojtyla, the Bishop of Krakow, became the first Eastern European Pope (and the first to hail from the Eastern bloc) upon his election as John Paul II in 1978. John Paul II visited Poland in early June 1979, drawing million-strong crowds. Soviet authorities stopped short of opposing his homecoming, leaving any decision on the matter to Polish authorities.

19 In 1980, Jerzy Popieluszko had agreed to conduct a mass at a Warsaw steel plant whose striking workers couldn't get to church. During the period of martial law, Popieluszko was actively involved in charity work and spoke out in support of defendants in political trials.

20 "Oblozhka" programme, Echo Moscow, March 4, 2015:http://echo.msk.ru/programs/oblozhka 1/1504176-echo/

21 *Perestroika* [Restructuring, in Russian] was the policy of restructuring the economic and political apparatus of the Soviet Union in the mid to late 1980s. The policy is associated with Mikhail Gorbachev, who, in May 1985, at a speech in Leningrad, publicly admitted that the economy was not doing well – that was a rare admission from a General Secretary of the Communist Party. At the 27th Congress of the CPSU held in February and March of 1986, Gorbachev developed the idea of reforming the planned economy, using words such as "perestroika" and "glasnost" [openness]. At this time, there was no thought about instituting a market economy.

Gorbachev himself referred back to the Prague Spring of 1968 in Czechoslovakia, as an influence on his thinking. In answer to a question what was the difference between *perestroika* and the Prague Spring, Gorbachev replied "nineteen years." But had he examined the way in which those earlier ideas of freedom had metamorphosed, much faster, and in more ways than Alexander Dubček had ever imagined, Gorbachev might have understood that he was lighting a touchpaper, which would lead to the revolutions in Eastern Europe in 1989, the dissolution of the Soviet Union in 1991, and the end of the Cold War.

22 The Round Table Talks took place in Warsaw, from February 6 to April 5 1989. It was primarily fear of social disturbances arising from an economic depression that caused the Communist government under Jaruzelski to begin talks with the banned, but powerful Solidarity trade union. The Communists were hoping to somehow bring Solidarity into the existing power structure, but without instituting any structural reforms. In practice, the talks revealed the general bankruptcy of the Jaruzelski regime, and soon led to a Solidarity government.

23 *Société des Jacobins, amis de la liberté et de l'égalité*, popularly known as the *Club des Jacobin*s, hence Jacobins, was the most influential republican political club during the French Revolution, with a membership of some half a million.

The club took its name from its Paris location, the Dominican convent in the Rue St Jacques (Latin: Jacobus). Members came from all sides of the political spectrum, from the radical Mountain, led by Robespierre, to the moderate Girondists, led by Brissot.

Revolutionary France in 1792-3 was governed first by the Girondists, but when they lost the support of the public, in May 1793, they were removed in a coup d'etat supported by the National Guard. Robespierre came to power, simultaneously introducing progressive legislation – universal suffrage was one – and the Reign of Terror, during which many Girondists (and generally anybody else Robespierre didn't like) were guillotined. When Robespierre fell in July 1794, it was the end of the Jacobins, and the Jacobin Club was closed.

Since then, the term "Jacobin(s)" has been used to characterise any radical left-wing politician or group.

24 The Polish parliamentary elections of 1989 were partially free: there was full-scale competition for seats in the upper house (Senate) only. Solidarity secured a landslide victory, winning 99 of the 100 seats (the only non-Solidarity being businessman Henrik Stoklosy, who had stood as an independent candidate). In the lower-house (Sejm) elections, however, Solidarity was allowed by election law to put forward candidates for only 35% of seats, all of which were won.

25 Chekists, from Cheka (Russian: ЧК – чрезвычайная комиссия, *chrezvychaynaya komissiya*, Emergency Committee), the first Soviet state security organisation, created end 1917. Under its first (and ruthless) leader Felix Dzerzhinsky, a Polish aristocrat turned communist, the Cheka expanded all across Russia. As late as the 1980s anybody connected to a security structure might be referred to as a "Chekist." "Chekist" is still used as a term for those with connections to the security agencies (quite proudly by some).

26 Ministry for State Security (German: *Ministerium für Staatssicherheit*) commonly known as the Stasi, was the official state security service of the German Democratic Republic (GDR), or "East Germany." At home, it spied on the population, relying on a nationwide network of informers, and suppressing by any means all dissent; abroad, it was a highly effective information-gathering operation, promoting communism, and countering capitalism.

27 Gorbachev denies any role in the dispersal of demonstrations in Tbilisi and the storming of the television centre in Vilnius.

28 *Glasnost* (Russian: Гласность, meaning "openness"), is today associated largely with the period 1986-1991 when Mikhail Gorbachev was calling for more transparency, and less corruption, in the Soviet government and its institutions. But it was not intended as a mechanism for ending the rule of the Communist Party, nor for instituting a capitalist, free-markey economy, although that is what the policy led to.

Glasnost was not a term invented by Gorbachev, for it had been in use since the late 18th century, when its meaning was closer to that of "public knowledge" of the workings of government. A century later, the meaning had developed, encompassing the right of the public to attend court hearings.

In view of what *Glasnost* ultimately came to mean, it is ironic that the word was revived by Soviet dissidents. On December 5, 1965, shortly before the Sinyavsky-Daniel trial, protestors gathered in Pushkin Square, central Moscow, demanding an "open trial" (*glasny sud*), a protest that became known as the *Glasnost* Meeting. In 1975, Andrei Sakharov stood outside a courthouse in Vilnius demanding access to the trial of Sergei Kovalyov, the human rights activist. Only ten years later, Gorbachev, General Secretary of the Communist Party, was using the same word, if not with the meaning as understood by dissidents, then with enough fluidity of interpretation to help bring down the system he had only been looking to reform.

29 The lustration process in Czechoslovakia, set in motion by legislation passed in 1991-92, was directed against members of the Communist Party of Czechoslovakia

(the ruling party between 1948 and 1989) as well as government intelligence agents and their collaborators. Individuals proven to have collaborated with the secret police were barred from holding public office for five years. In Poland, mass lustration began in 1997. Candidates for senior government positions, including elected positions, were obliged to present reliable evidence of their activities prior to 1989; failure to do so resulted in a ten-year ban from public office.

30 The so-called Michnik Commission conducted research in the archives of the Ministry of Internal Affairs between April 12 and June 27, 1990. The Commission aimed to verify the integrity of the archives and the reliability of the documents. It comprised the New Acts Archive director Bogdan Kroll (Chair); historian Jerzy Holzer; historian and Academy of Sciences member Andrzej Ajnenkiel; and historian, Gazeta Wyborcza editor and Sejm deputy Adam Michnik. The Commission produced a two-page report detailing the unsatisfactory condition of the archives and the incompleteness and unreliability of the documents therein.

31 The UN Convention against Corruption was adopted in 2003. The Russian Federation ratified the Convention in 2006 but failed to include Article 20, which introduced the notion of "illicit enrichment." Illicit enrichment thus remains uncriminalised in Russia. In 2014, Alexei Navalny's Anti-Corruption Foundation collected 100,000 online signatures for a petition calling for the ratification of Article 20, but the bill was never considered by the State Duma.

32 The first rumours concerning Lech Wałęsa's cooperation with the security services had emerged as early as the mid-1970s. Wałęsa himself denies any such claims. In 2000, the lustration court failed to find any documentary proof that the Security Service had co-opted Wałęsa. But in 2008, historians from the Institute of National Memory presented a multitude of documents that *did* offer evidence of cooperation. It is probable that the arrested Wałęsa was indeed forced to sign a cooperation agreement following the violent suppression of the unrest in Gdansk in December 1970, but it remains unclear whether genuine cooperation subsequently took place.

33 The notion of the "thick line" (*gruba kreska*) was introduced by Prime Minister Tadeusz Mazowiecki in a speech to the Sejm on August 24, 1989: "The government we are creating is not responsible for the legacy of the old regime. [...] We will bear responsibility only for what we have done in order to guide the country out of the present catastrophic situation."

34 Michnik is referring to Yemelyan Pugachev (c. 1742 –1775), self-styled pretender to the Russian throne, who was the leader of, and gave his name to the Pugachev Rebellion (also known as the Cossack Rebellion) of 1773-75, the largest peasant revolt in Russia's history.

Russia, under Catherine II, was at war with the Ottoman Empire, which, as so often, soon caused peasant disturbances. The Yaik Cossacks, led by Pugachev (a former lieutenant in Catherine's army), agitating for independence, took the lead in the revolt. Displaying considerable military skill, and having taken Kazan in July 1774, Pugachev and his motley band (of peasants, Old Believers and Cossacks) were soon in control of a large area between the Volga River and the Urals.

Taking advantage of the official government's military disarray, and the initial failure of Catherine's administration to understand the seriousness of the situation, Pugachev formed an alternative government in the name of the late Tsar Peter III (Catherine's former husband who had been assassinated by her followers). Pugachev was clever enough to proclaim an end to serfdom, which cemented his popularity, but was undone by increasing delusions of grandeur (he said that he *was* Peter III), and the recovery of the Catherine government.

In August 1774, at Tsaritsyn, the revolt was crushed by General Michelsohn. The "Marquis de Pugachev," as Catherine, relieved, now referred to him, was given up by his own supporters, and executed on Bolotnaya Square in Moscow, in January 1775.

The revolt has remained in the minds of Russians primarily because of Pushkin's *The Captain's Daughter* (1836), which is set during the rebellion. *Pugachevschina* ["Time of Pugachev"], as a term, is used to describe the supposedly innate urge to rebel in the Russian people.

35 In December 1985, Boris Yeltsin replaced Victor Grishin as the First Secretary of the Moscow Party Committee. Yeltsin's leadership style was radically different from Grishin's: he engaged actively with Muscovites, organised unscheduled inspection visits to factories and businesses, and talked to the press, thus reducing the distance between the *nomenklatura* and

society at large in a manner that was fully consistent with the spirit of Gorbachev's *perestroika*. However, Yeltsin also permitted himself to level criticism at Gorbachev and Politburo members who were hindering the processes of *perestroika*. Yelstin's condemnations of the slow pace at which *perestroika* was proceeding earned him adulation and support across the country, and helped him become party oppositionist No. 1 in the RSFSR.

36 Yegor Gaidar (1956–2009), Soviet-Russian economist, politician, acting Prime Minister of Russia from 15 June 1992 to 14 December 1992, was the principal architect of the "Shock Therapy" reform programme of the early 1990s, which attempted to rapidly turn the planned economy of the Soviet Union into a market economy.

Gaidar still divides Russians even today, many of whom blame him for the loss of their savings (because of hyperinflation) and the failure to prevent large chunks of the privatised economy from falling into the hands of a small group of well-connected businessmen, vilified as "oligarchs" and "kleptocrats." There are others, however, with a more favourable viewpoint, such as the late Boris Nemtsov, who declared that he averted civil war; and Mikhail Khodorkovsky who stated that "[Gaidar] laid the foundation of our economy."

37 Anatoly Chubais (1955-), responsible for privatisation in the Yeltsin government. A native of St Petersburg, in the 1980s he was a noted proponent of economic reform in the city, meeting many people with whom he would later work, including Anatoly Sobchak and Yegor Gaidar. It was Chubais who implemented the

much-criticised voucher privatisation programme (signed into law by President Yeltsin on August 19, 1992), which gave all Russians who chose to pay a minimal fee a voucher that could be used to buy a stake in one of the country's state enterprises, most of which were required to sell about 29 percent of their shares to the public in a "voucher auction." Amid hyperinflation in 1992-3, many Russians sold their vouchers on the market for about $20. The programme became highly unpopular when, some years later, entrepreneurs who had bought up the vouchers and invested them wisely, ended up holding stakes worth billions of dollars.

38 The All-Union Leninist Young Communist League (popularly known as "Komsomol," a shortening of *kommunisticheskii soyuz molodyozhi*) was the political youth wing of the Soviet Communist Party. Membership was not officially compulsory, but membership was understood to be the first rung of an official career; and not to become a member was to mark oneself out as different, which was enough to merit unwelcome attention from the authorities.

39 Donald Tusk was one of the founders of the liberal magazine *Przegląd polityczny* (*The Political Review*), published clandestinely between 1983 and1989; the magazine "contributed to the emergence of Polish liberalism as an ideological current" (See L.S. Lykoshina, *Donald Tusk: A Political Portrait* [Moscow: INION RAN, 2013]). The centre-right Liberal-Democratic Congress party, founded in 1990, enjoyed modest success in the 1991 Sejm elections, but was trounced in 1993.

40 Michnik is referring to the apartment bombings in Moscow and Volgodonsk in September 1999.

41 The K-141 Kursk submarine sank on August 12, 2000 while taking part in a naval exercise in the Barents Sea. President Putin was on holiday in Sochi at the time, and broke off his vacation only on the sixth day of the disaster. Putin refused to take responsibility for what happened, blaming the tragedy on the "chaos" reigning in the country throughout the previous fifteen years. In September of the same year Putin gave an interview to Larry King while on a visit to the USA. When asked what had befallen the submarine, he replied, "It sank."

42 One of Russia's most popular independent TV channels during the 1990s, NTV was taken over by Gazprom in 2000, the likely reason for the takeover being the channel's support for the "Fatherland – All Russia" electoral bloc, the main rival to the pro-government Unity Party in the parliamentary elections of 1999. According to NTV insiders, the primary reason was rather NTV's objective coverage of the war in Chechnya, which flared up again in August 1999.

43 Ukraine's Orange Revolution of 2004 comprised a series of protests by supporters of presidential candidate Viktor Yushchenko. The protests began after the Central Election Commission announced the preliminary results of the second round of the presidential election on November 21, with Yushchenko's opponent Viktor Yanukovych declared the winner. The epicentre of the revolution was Kiev's main square, the Maidan, where a many-thousands-strong protest of indefinite duration began on November 22. The Orange

revolution grew into a regional political crisis whose resolution came to involve representatives from Russia, Poland, Lithuania and the EU. The protesters succeeded in forcing the nullification of the second-round results by the Supreme Court on December 3. Yushchenko claimed victory following a revote on December 26. According to many political analysts, the Orange Revolution exerted a profound influence on the evolution of the political regime in Russia.

44 A reference to Grinyov's words in Pushkin's short novel *The Captain's Daughter* (published 1836, about the Pugachev Rebellion of 1773-5), "May God preserve us from a witnessing a Russian rebellion, meaningless and merciless."

45 *Landmarks* (1909) and *From the Depths* (1918) were anthologies of essays penned by Russian philosophers (Semyon Frank, Peter Struve, Nikolai Berdyaev, Sergei Bulgakov, Alexander Isgoyev, Mikhail Gershenzon, *et al.*), the former dealing with the revolutions of 1905-07 and the latter with those of 1917, and both examining the role played by the intelligentsia.

46 The National Bolshevik Party (Russian: Национал-большевистская партия) is a political group (it was never officially registered as a party) espousing National Bolshevism. In existence since 1994, and led by Eduard Limonov, the group, which has sheltered many opposing factions, came to prominence for its public "stone throwing," (the title of its newspaper *Limonka*, plays both on the founder's surname and the slang word for a grenade) protesting against an often bewildering catalogue of dislikes – anti-Putin, anti-

corruption, anti-authoritarian. The group has been tainted with accusations of fascist tendencies. In 2010, Limonov founded a new party, The Other Russia.

47 The Law and Justice Party (PiS) was founded by the brothers Lech and Jaroslaw Kaczyński in 2001. Its ideology is rooted in conservatism, solidarism, Christian democracy, and euroscepticism. The party won an overall majority in the 2015 parliamentary election.

48 Janusz Korwin-Mikke is a notorious Polish populist politician and the creator of several conservative-liberal political parties (the Real Politics Union, the Congress of the New Right, and KORWIN). Korwin-Mikke is a eurosceptic. In the 2014 European Parliament elections, his New Right won 4 of Poland's 51 seats. In 2015, Janusz Korwin-Mikke was expelled from the party and founded the right-libertarian and eurosceptic KORWiN (*Koalicja Odnowy Rzeczypospolitej Wolność i Nadzieja*) – the Coalition for the Renewal of the Republic – Liberty and Hope.

49 Named after Viktor Orbán (1963-), Hungarian politician. Prime Minister since 2010 (and 1998-2002), and president of Fidesz, the ruling national conservative party. His rule has been characterised by an increasingly strident and authoritarian rule, hence "orbánisation."

50 The complex of radical economic reforms known as "shock therapy" was implemented in Poland under Finance Minister Leszek Balcerowicz ("Balcerowicz Plan") from 1990 onwards, and in Russia under acting Prime Minister Yegor Gaidar from 1992 onwards. In

both cases, the reformers were guided by a set of policy recommendations from Western economists and financial institutions sometimes referred to as the "Washington Consensus." The proposed measures included price and foreign-trade liberalisation, a tough monetary policy, strict budgetary discipline, privatisation, and so forth. The reforms were followed by a sharp decline in living standards that some attributed to mistakes made by the reformers and others to the legacy of the Soviet system and the macroeconomic imbalances accumulated during the Gorbachev period.

51 Per World Bank estimates: Poland's per capita GDP (PPP) in 1990 was $5966 (international dollars in 2013 prices) – $2047 dollars less than that of the RSFSR ($8013). In 2011, Poland marginally overtook Russia: the countries' figures for that year were $21,260 and $21,245 respectively. And while Russia's increase owed much to a sharp rise in the price of oil, its main export commodity, that of Poland owed more to increased productivity.

52 Presidential Decree No. 1400 was issued by Yeltsin on September 21, 1993. The decree suspended the activities of the Supreme Council of the Russian Federation, which, in the eyes of the president, was hindering the implementation of vitally important socio-economic reforms and exceeding its jurisdiction by interfering in the affairs of the executive and the judiciary.

53 Boris Yeltsin (1931-2007). Soviet-Russian politician, first President of the Russian Federation (1991-1999). Starting out as a Gorbachev supporter, he became an opponent, unhappy with what he saw as the slow pace

of reform. His resignation from the Politburo in 1987 caused him to be seen as a man of the people.

As president, Yeltsin faced significant establishment opposition, which came to a head in the 1993 constitutional crisis. Yeltsin ordered the dissolution of the Supreme Soviet parliament which then attempted to remove him from office. In October of that year, troops loyal to Yeltsin put down an armed revolt, outside the parliament building (the Russian "White House"). Yeltsin did away with the then constitution, and called an election for three months later. 12 parties were allowed to run, many of them opposition parties, including the Communists and Zhirinovsky's LDPR, which came first in the list voting. Yeltsin banned some groups directly involved in the uprising and newspapers that directly supported it, but resisted calls to ban opposition groups.

His re-election in 1996 was marred by corruption and electoral fraud. Ultimately, his popularity was destroyed by the economic crises that beset Russia in the 1990s, caused both by low oil and commodity prices, and the rapid transformation of the country from a planned economy to a free-market one, which, although it opened up opportunities for private enterprise, soon gave control of major parts of the economy to a small number of businessmen, whose wealth and power led to their being called the "oligarchs." On 31 December 1999, Yeltsin announced his resignation, leaving the presidency in the hands of his chosen successor, the little-known prime minister Vladimir Putin.

54 The article in question ("Law – And Nothing But Law") was published in *Rossiyskaya Gazeta* on March 24, 2015: "The fact is that Yeltsin's decree No. 1400,

which you so ardently support, set a precedent for the crudest possible interpretation of constitutional law (or rather its virtual revocation) in one of the world's key countries. And it was not for nothing that this precedent came to be greeted so enthusiastically almost everywhere in the West, and declared a just solution to the political problem at hand. For it is precisely this precedent that has been appropriated by your fellow-thinkers in the West as the new and permissible norm. Which, depending on the exigencies of context, is dubbed either 'democracy is more important than the law' or 'justice is more important than the law'. In any case, the law is not the priority [...] You must realise that it is precisely due to the precedent set by decree No. 1400 [...] that the methodologies and technologies of the various 'coloured revolutions' have burgeoned." The text is available on the newspaper's official website: http://www.rg.ru/2015/03/23/zorkin-site.html.

55 Lee Kuan Yew provides a detailed account of anti-corruption efforts in Singapore in his memoir *From Third World to First: The Singapore Story, 1965-2000*.

56 Rzeszów is the administrative centre of Podkarpackie Voivodeship. The city is home to three higher-education institutions: Rzeszow University, The Polytechnic University, and the University of Information Technology and Management.

57 A reference to the Great Purge of 1936-38, also known as the Great Terror, a systematic campaign of repression and executions ordered by Stalin. Between 600,000 to 1.2 million people – Communist and government officials, Red Army personnel, and peas-

ants – were murdered. The most brutal period from 1937-8 is known as the *Yezhovshchina* ("Time of Yezhov"), named after Nikolai Yezhov, head of the NKVD secret police. As a name, the Soviet Great Terror alludes to the Reign of Terror, during the French Revolution, which lasted from June to July 1794.

58 Václav Havel, "The Power of the Powerless" (excerpt): "It seems that the primary breeding ground for what might, in the widest possible sense of the word, be understood as an *opposition in the post-totalitarian* system is living within the truth. [...] For the crust presented by the life of lies is made of strange stuff. As long as it seals off hermetically the entire society, it appears to be made of stone. But the moment someone breaks through in one place, when one person cries out, 'The emperor is naked!', when a single person breaks the rules of the game, thus exposing it as a game, everything suddenly appears in another light and the whole crust seems then to be made of a tissue on the point of tearing and disintegrating uncontrollably" [tr. Paul Wilson].

59 A reference to Václav Havel's 1991 interview with Adam Michnik: "In my latest book I claim that, in certain regions of the world at least, there's real hope of putting an end to the era of ideologies and embarking upon an era of ideas. This would be the era of the open society, the era of global connections and global responsibilities. At the same time, this should also be the era of non-doctrinal ways of thinking. […] I don't understand what [the term 'worldview'] actually means. Is the world really simple enough for you to have a single global viewpoint on it? I have a thousand different contradictory views on different things, a

thousand different opinions. Pluralistic thinking prevents conflicts in the best possible way. For at the heart of any conflict – be it rooted in ideology, class or nationality – is a divergence of monolithic worldviews."

60 The notion of "sovereign democracy" was advanced circa 2005-2006 by Vladislav Surkov, Deputy Chief of the Presidential Administration. As defined by Surkov, sovereign democracy constituted "a form of political life of society, under which the authorities, their organs and actions are selected, formed and directed exclusively by the Russian nation in all its variety and completeness so that all citizens, social groups and peoples comprising it achieve material well-being, freedom and justice" (V. Surkov, Nationalization of the Future // Expert 43 (537), 2006). [Translation quoted here: *Developments in Russian Politics 7*, ed. Stephen White, Richard Sakwa, Henry E. Hale, p. 14 <Google Books>] In practice, the notion of sovereign democracy has become an ideological smokescreen for authoritarianism: restriction of civil liberties, establishment of control over the media, and so on.

61 Denis Volkov, sociologist, Levada Centre expert: "Twelve months on, attitudes to the annexation of Crimea remain positive: 88% welcomed the annexation in March 2014, and, a year later, that percentage remains unchanged. However, conceptions of what would constitute an acceptable development in the situation in Eastern Ukraine have changed significantly. In March 2014, 74% of respondents were prepared to support the Russian government in the eventuality of open military conflict between the two countries; by February 2015, however, that number had

decreased to 44%. Views on the desirable future of the eastern territories have changed as well: in 2014, 48% of respondents believed that they should be incorporated into Russia, as compared to a mere 15% in 2015" (http://carnegie.ru/2015/07/02/ru-60582/ibli).

62 Elections to the Board of Deputies in the newly created municipality of Balashikha and Zheleznodorozhny (Moscow Region) were held on April 26, 2015. An alliance of independent observers remarked in a press release of the same day that "voting ended at 20:00. Immediately prior to that time, or immediately after, unknown individuals dressed in sports gear arrived at several polling stations and took active part in the counting of ballots, threatening independent monitors with physical violence and saying they would 'smash their heads in' and 'wring their necks.'" (http://www.golosinfo.org/ru/articles/1653).

63 According to the Russian Academy of Sciences' Institute of Sociology, a majority of Russians believe that leading world-power status may be achieved by dint of a high level of economic development (58%) and of citizens' wellbeing (53%), as well as by the condition of the armed forces (44%). An ever-growing number of respondents are underscoring the importance of the country's cultural and spiritual life (up from 23% in 2005 to 39% in 2014). In contrast, any "messianic" elements of the country's greatness are deemed significant only by a minority of respondents. Meanwhile, the number of respondents in favour of the reintegration of post-Soviet space has declined from 14% in 2005 to 8% in 2014.

64 Osip Mandelstam was born in Warsaw in 1891. In

2012, Warsaw became the first city in the world to immortalise the poet in a street name.

65 *For the thundering glory of the coming ages,*
For the tall race of men,
I've given up my cup at my father's feast,
And my joy, and my honour.

The wolf-fanged century leaps at my shoulders,
But my blood isn't a wolf's blood,
So, like a crumpled hat, stuff me into the sleeve,
Of a Siberian sheepskin,

So I won't have to see the cowards, nor the bits of gristle,
The bloody bones stuck in the wheel,
So all night the polar foxes may shine
On me in their primordial beauty.

Take me into the night where the Yenisei flows,
Where the pine tops touch the stars,
Because my blood isn't a wolf's blood,
And only an equal will kill me.

Osip Mandelstam
17-18 March 1931, end of 1935
Translated by Alex Halberstadt

66 The Catholic Church, supported by conservatives, proposed including a provision concerning the innate religiosity of the Poles (*Invocatio Dei*) in the new Polish Constitution (1997), but encountered strong opposition from left-wingers and liberals. As a result, the following formula, which merely *references* God (*Nominatio Dei*), was adopted instead: "We, the Polish nation, all citizens

of the Republic, both those who believe in God as the source of truth, justice, good and beauty, as well as those not sharing such faith but respecting those universal values as arising from other sources, equal in rights and obligations towards the common good of Poland […]."

67 In his book *Neighbours* (2000), Jan Tomasz Gross describes the massacre of the Jewish population of the village of Jedwabne, which took place on July 10, 1941. The massacre differs from other Holocaust atrocities in Poland in the sense that its architects were not Nazis but Poles – literally the neighbours of local Jews. Gross' book catalysed the most far-reaching historical debate in Poland's recent history. Far from everyone was willing to accept the fact that it was Poles, albeit directed by the Germans, who perpetrated the massacre. In an interview with Mikhail Fishman for Slon.ru in 2015, Gross commented that "society is mostly in a state of denial [regarding the Holocaust in Poland], as evidenced by opinion polls […]. As polls demonstrate, a majority of people believe that the Poles suffered more during the war than the Jews. Something like 30% would say that this isn't the case and are ready to accept the facts." (Https://slon.ru/posts/53286).

68 Self-Defence of the Republic of Poland was a left-nationalist populist party founded by controversial politician Andrzej Lepper. In 2006, the party entered into a coalition with the PiS and the League of Polish Families – a right-wing Catholic nationalist party. After the collapse of the coalition in 2007, the latter was forced into the margins of Polish political life, while Self-Defence of the Republic of Poland all but ceased to exist after Lepper's suicide in 2011.

69 The presidential Tu-154 crashed near Smolensk on April 10, 2010, killing Lech Kaczynski, his wife and 94 prominent Polish leaders. According to the findings of the Interstate Aviation Committee, the crash occurred because the poorly trained crew was unable to cope with rapidly deteriorating weather conditions. The Civic Platform party accepted the outcome of the investigation. Law and Justice, led by the deceased president's twin brother Jaroslaw Kaczyński, entertains the conspiracy theory that the disaster was concocted by the Russian government (acting either on its own initiative or in collusion with then Polish Prime Minister Donald Tusk, a political opponent of the Kaczyńskis).

70 After the Second World War, the new communist authorities seized more than 90% of the landholdings of the Catholic Church. In 1989, the Sejm passed a law regulating state-church relations, which featured a clause on the principles of restitution. The Property Commission, which was established pursuant to that law, returned 65,700 hectares and 490 buildings to the church as well as prescribing that it be paid compensation of 140 million zlotys for land and buildings that wouldn't be returned.

71 The ratification of the Council of Europe Convention on preventing and combating violence against women and domestic violence, and the determination of the legal status of in-vitro fertilisation (IVF) are the most controversial family- and marriage-related issues in modern Poland. Ratification and legalisation are opposed by right-wing conservative parties and religious groups. The church, meanwhile, threatens couples who resort to IVF, and the doctors who

perform it, with excommunication. Nevertheless, the political weight of those opposed to the convention and to IVF is not all that significant; the Convention was adopted in April 2015, before entering into force on August 1 of the same year; and in the summer of 2015, after eight years of fierce debate, a law making IVF available to both married and unmarried couples was approved as well.

72 Gallicanism is a set of religious, political and legal doctrines substantiating the autonomy of the French Catholic Church and its unaccountability to the Vatican on various questions. Gallicanism originated in the fourteenth and fifteenth centuries, and enjoyed a degree of popularity until the French Revolution.

73 In February 2012, the feminist punk band Pussy Riot staged "punk prayers" in two of Moscow's churches: Yelokhovo Cathedral and the Cathedral of Christ the Saviour.

74 In March 2012, three alleged members of the group – Nadezhda Tolokonnikova, Maria Alyokhina and Yekaterina Samutsevich – were arrested. On August 17, the Khamovniki District Court of Moscow sentenced the accused to two years in a penal colony. The Pussy Riot trial attracted the attention of the liberal community and the world's media.

75 Patriarch Kirill met Pope Francis on February 13, 2016 at Havana airport, Cuba. Part of the meeting was held in public; and for a few hours the two men spoke in private. A pre-prepared joint communiqué was issued.

76 A "Joint Message to the Peoples of Russia and Poland" was signed in August 2012, during Patriarch Kirill's first visit to the latter. The text of the document had a pronounced conciliatory character: "After the Second World War and the painful experience of atheism, which was imposed on our nations, today we enter a path of spiritual and material renewal. We call on our faithful to ask for the forgiveness of the wrongs, injustice and all evil we have inflicted on each other. We are confident that this is the first and foremost step to rebuild mutual trust, a precondition for a sustainable human community and complete reconciliation … Today our nations are faced with yet new challenges. Fundamental moral principles based on the Ten Commandments are questioned under the pretence of retaining the principle of secularism or the protection of freedom. We are faced with the promotion of abortion, euthanasia and same-sex relations, persistently shown as a form of marriage; a consumerist lifestyle is endorsed, traditional values rejected, while religious symbols are removed from public space. Quite often we encounter signs of hostility towards Christ, His Gospel and Cross; attempts are made to exclude the Church from public life. A misinterpreted secularism assumes a form of fundamentalism and in reality is a form of atheism." (The full text is available here: http://www.news.va/en/news/church-leaders-send-joint-message-to-poland-and-ru).

77 *Dissidents* (2014), a memoir by Aleksandr Podrabinek, (1953-). Soviet dissident, political prisoner; one of the founders of the Working Commission for the Investigation of the Use of Psychiatry for Political Purposes, during the Moscow–Helsinki group (1977).

78 The religious situation in the Russian Empire of the early twentieth century was extremely complex. The de facto established Russian Orthodox Church was in the midst of an acute crisis, a fact openly discussed by the participants of the religio-philosophical gatherings of 1901-1903. Against this background of crisis, a growing number of Orthodox adherents were being seduced by Old Ritualism and sectarianism. Estimates of their number vary from 2 million people (official statistics) to 20-25 million (as reckoned by certain contemporaries).

79 Scandals involving "offence to religious feelings" periodically flare up in Poland. For instance, a case involving former Sejm deputy and League of Polish Families member Witold Tomczak has been simmering with varying degrees of intensity for the last fifteen years. In 2000, a thoroughly scandalised Tomczak damaged *La Nona ora*, an installation by Italian artist Maurizio Cattelan being exhibited at Warsaw's *Zachęta* Gallery. *La Nona ora* depicted Pope John Paul II struck down by a meteorite.

80 In April 2015, three women out of a group of six were filmed twerking in front of the Malaya Zemlya monument to the Second World War in Novorossiysk, southern Russia, and subsequently jailed for hooliganism. Prosecutors said that "This incident of disrespect for the memory of war history is unacceptable and any attempts to desecrate sites of military glory will be stopped immediately." Two of the women were jailed for ten days and the third for fifteen days.

81 In March 2015, St Petersburg hosted the International

Russian Conservative Forum, which was attended by Europe's right- and ultra-right-wingers. Commentators noted the complete absence of moderate conservatives, and the abundance of fascist or semi-fascist parties: Germany's National Democrats, Italy's New Force, Greece's Golden Dawn, the British National Party, and others.

82 Ernst Röhm (1887-1934). German military officer, founding member of the Nazi Party. He had made friends with Adolph Hitler when they had both been members of the German Workers' Party. He co-founded the Sturmabteilun, (English: Storm Battalion), the Nazi militia, becoming its commander. Hitler came to see him as a rival, and he was executed during the "Night of the Long Knives," when, from June 30 to July 1, Hitler ordered the killing of many of his enemies.

83 The notion of "people's democracy" emerged after the Second World War and was used to describe the pro-Soviet regimes of (South-)Eastern Europe and East Asia. From a Marxist/Communist point of view, unlike "bourgeois democracy," where the real power was wielded by the class of exploiters, the power in people's democracies belonged to yesterday's exploited, i.e., the working people. However, people's democracies were regarded as societally immature and as having only just embarked on the road to socialism.

84 "Imitation democracy" is a term used to refer to political regimes that possess all the requisite democratic infrastructure but do not function as true democracies in practice; the rule of law exists in name alone. There is no genuine "level playing field" for the various

participants of the political process; speech is free merely to the extent prescribed by the government; and electoral mechanisms function in such a way that only "acceptable" parties and candidates ever emerge triumphant.

85 The January Uprising began on January 22, 1863, ending in 1864 with the capture of the last rebels.

The catalyst was the weakening of Imperial Russia after it lost the Crimean War. In 1861, patriotic demonstrations broke out in the former Polish-Lithuanian Commonwealth (present-day Poland, Lithuania, Belarus, Latvia, western and northern Ukraine, and western Russia). In Vilnius there were more than a hundred protests, characterised by nationalist rhetoric. A State of Emergency was declared in some regions, leading to martial law in Poland in October 1861.

At a series of meetings held across Europe, the outlawed leaders split into two factions: the Reds, largely made up of peasants and workers, and the Whites, of liberal landowners and intellectuals.

The immediate cause of the revolt was a protest by young Poles against conscription into the Imperial Russian Army, who were soon joined by Polish-Lithuanian officers. Heavily outnumbered, poorly equipped and provisioned, and unable to decisively win a pitched battle (though hundreds of these did take place), the rebels used what we would now call guerrilla tactics.

The rebel provisional government (of Reds and Whites) issued a stirring call for help, and in a manifesto declared that "all sons of Poland are free and equal citizens without distinction of creed, condition and rank." It offered land to the peasants, and compensation to landlords. This was enough to ignite a popular revolt, for which there was widespread public support across Europe.

The European powers sensed an opportunity to weaken Russia, and a general anti-Russian coalition seemed to be in the offing, but Alexander III acted decisively, forestalling any wider action against him.

Under Mikhail Muravyov ("the hangman"), Russia ruthlessly put down the rising, hanging some, deporting thousands, burning whole towns and villages.

Russia then systematically destroyed the *szlachta*, the Polish nobility, dispossessing landlords that had taken part in or supported the revolt, and giving land to the peasants. Russian became the official language, and Poland lost its former autonomy, with the country divided into provinces under a Russian Governor-General.

86 The Polish-Russian small border traffic (*maly ruch graniczny*) agreement came into force in July 2012. Traffic is relatively intense in both directions: in August 2014, the border was crossed by 328,000 non-visa-bearing individuals. The sharp drop in the rouble in the autumn of the same year had a negative impact on cross-border traffic: by February 2015, volume had plummeted by over 50% to 150,000 people, before starting to rise again.

87 The idea of a "return to Europe" materialised in the 1970s. Its originators were Václav Havel, Adam Michnik, György Konrad, and others. The idea was rooted in the belief that the Second World War had precipitated a seismic shift in the cultural and political landscape of Europe: the European East, associated with the Soviet Union prior to the war, absorbed

Central and Eastern Europe and, as such, Central Europe lost its identity. After the war, Europe was rent into East and West, the Iron Curtain cleaving the continent in two. The "real" Europe was in the West, where all the values of European culture had been preserved intact. Hungary, Poland and Czechoslovakia, which, together with Germany and Austria, comprised the core of what was once Central Europe, became quasi-colonies of the Soviet Union, and were excised from the European cultural space.

The preservation of "European-ness" in (post-) totalitarian conditions was therefore regarded by Hungarian, Polish and Czechoslovak dissidents as the first of two preeminent challenges, the second being the reintegration of their respective countries into the "real" Europe at the earliest opportunity. In 1991, shortly after the "velvet revolutions," the leaders of Hungary, Poland and Czechoslovakia gathered in Visegrád, Hungary, and signed an agreement to cooperate on European integration issues.

88 The famous Brodsky-Kundera polemic took place in January 1985 on the book review pages of the *New York Times*. The Czech contrasted the work of the French Enlightenment *philosophe* Denis Diderot with that of Fyodor Dostoyevsky, whose writings he regarded as the very quintessence of the Russian mentality. Irrational by nature and dominated by feeling, the latter, according to Kundera, was alien to the mentality of the post-Enlightenment West. Brodsky, for his part, vigorously disputed Kundera's "handy dichotomies of feeling-reason, Dostoevsky-Diderot, them-us."

89 In July 2014, two international bodies – the European Court of Human Rights and the Hague Tribunal – decreed that the Russian Federation must pay compensation to the shareholders of Yukos, whose assets had effectively been expropriated by the Russian state. The Hague Tribunal found that the shareholders are entitled to compensation as per Article 13 of the Energy Charter Treaty, which Russia signed in 1999 but refused to ratify in 2009. After Russian assets were seized in Belgium, France and Austria in June 2015, President Putin declared that Russia would not recognise the decision of the Hague Tribunal because its jurisdiction did not extend to countries that had not ratified the treaty.

90 The debate between Westerners and Slavophiles, which originated in the late 1830s, hinged on the two movements' respective conceptions of Russia's civilisational belonging. The Westerners, whose ranks included Pavel Annenkov, Timofei Granovsky, Konstantin Kavelin, Boris Chicherin and Vasily Botkin, argued that Russia had been following the Western path of development since at least the era of Peter I, and would therefore ultimately evolve into a constitutional monarchy or republic, which would ensure a consequent degree of societal progress. As their ideological opponents, the Slavophiles (Ivan and Konstantin Aksakov, Ivan and Peter Kireevsky, Alexander Koshelev, Yuri Samarin, Alexey Khomyakov) said that all the problems facing contemporary Russia were rooted precisely in the fact that Peter I disrupted the natural course of the country's development, which it had been following in "its own special way" until the end of the seventeenth century. Thus emerged one of the central

dichotomies of Russian philosophy and political thought – the "Western path" versus the "special path."

91 The term *Sonderweg* refers to the doctrine of Imperial Germany's own "special path," as distinct from Anglo-French bourgeois democracy and Russian Tsarism. After the Second World War, the notion of the *Sonderweg* became a historiographical construct used to explain the collapse of the democratic Weimar Republic and the triumph of National Socialism.

92 The Great Reforms of Alexander II – a response to Russia's defeat in the Crimean War (1853-56) – included: the emancipation of the serfs (1861); the introduction of local self-government for rural districts (1864) and urban areas (1870); an overhaul of the judicial system (1864); and military modernisation (1862-1874).

93 By the middle of the nineteenth century, various Polish stereotypes had crystallised in Russian literature; largely consonant with Poles' stereotypes of themselves, these included "properties of temperament (passion, impetuousness, cheerfulness, love of pleasure, proneness to enthusiasm); psychological makeup (impulsiveness, fickleness); and [...] moral qualities (acquiescence, levity, irresponsibility, anarchic tendencies)." See Leskinen, Maria, "The Polish Disposition in Russian Nineteenth-Century Ethnography", in *Notes of the Fatherland*, 2014, No. 4(61), p. 120.

94 Gustlik and Janek: Literary characters from the book *Four Tank-Men and a Dog* by Janusz Przymanowski; and known to Soviet children from the eponymous TV series.

95 The "Polish plumber" is a phrase first used in 2004 by Frits Bolkestein, the then-European Comissioner for Internal Market and Services, while discussing the liberalisation of the services market in the EU. Opponents of liberalisation (mainly socialists and trade union representatives) feared that it would lead to an influx of cheap Central- and Eastern-European labour (symbolised by the "Polish plumber") into Western Europe.

96 On September 17, 1939, the Red Army invaded Poland from the east. Over the course of the autumn campaign, several thousand Polish officers were taken prisoner by the Soviets and held in special camps near Smolensk, Ostashkov and Kharkov. In the spring of 1940, the Soviet leadership took the decision to eliminate the captured officers. According to statistics reported by KGB chief Alexander Shelepin to Nikita Khrushchev in 1959, a total of 21,857 people were shot, including 4421 in the Katyn Forest near Smolensk region. The USSR formally admitted responsibility for the Katyn massacre only in 1989. In 2010, classified documents containing definitive proof of the Soviet leadership's guilt in the matter were handed over to the Poles by Russian President Dmitry Medvedev (these are available on the website of the Federal Archive Agency: http://www.rusarchives.ru/publication/katyn/spisok.shtml).

97 The Warsaw Uprising of 1944 was an attempt by the Polish resistance and Home Army (Polish: *Armia Krajowa*) to liberate Warsaw from Nazi control. Launched on August 1 to coincide with the approach of Soviet forces on the eastern side of the city, Polish

forces fought for 63 days, but found themselves with little outside support, which allowed the Germans to regroup, and raze the city to the ground.

Stalin's lukewarm support (the Soviets remained beyond the city limits, and gave little or no air support) was likely a political calculation designed to foil the attempt by the Polish Underground State to form an independent Poland, allow the Nazis to destroy the resistance, and thus leave the field open to the Soviet-backed Polish Committee of National Liberation.

Winston Churcill, who sent 200 supply drops from the UK, tried hard to persuade Stalin and Roosevelt to help, but Stalin refused to allow Western planes to land at Soviet bases; and the US sent only one airdrop.

Some 16,000 members of the Polish resistance were killed (the numbers are estimates) and 6,000 wounded. Up to 200,000 Polish civilians were killed and executed. German casualties totalled over 8,000 soldiers, with 9,000 wounded.

98 The Volhynia massacres were part of an ethnic cleansing operation directed against the local Polish population, carried out by the Ukrainian Insurgent Army in Volhynia and other areas of Western Ukraine in 1943-45.

99 Malaysia Airlines Flight 17 aircraft crashed en route from Amsterdam to Kuala Lumpur near the village of Hrabovo (60km east of Donetsk) on July 17, 2014, killing all 298 people on board. The Ukrainian authorities delegated the investigation of the disaster to the Netherlands. According to the investigation team's preliminary report, published in September 2014, the crash was not caused by technical defects and/or

piloting errors. The final report, released by the Dutch Safety Board in October of the following year, confirmed the already widespread theory that the plane was downed by a Russian-made Buk surface-to-air missile launched from Eastern Ukraine.

100 A reference to the Polish support of the Ukrainian People's Republic during the Ukrainian War of Independence 1917-1921. In return for military assistance, the beleaguered republic, led by Symon Petliura, fighting against the Soviet Bolsheviks (themselves fighting against the White Army), gave up both territory and some sovereignty. A bewildering series of victories and reversals for all sides finally led to the signing of a treaty in November 1921 between Poland and Soviet Russia, which effectively partitioned Ukraine, between the Bolshevik-controlled Ukrainian Soviet Socialist Republic, Poland, Romania and Czechoslovakia.

101 In 1947, Polish émigré Jerzy Giedroyc began publishing *Kultura*, a magazine that soon became a hotbed for Polish socio-political thought. Published initially in Rome and subsequently in Paris, *Kultura* was illegally distributed in Poland. Jerzy Giedroyc and Juliusz Meroshevsky, a well-known journalist and regular contributor to the magazine, played a key role in debunking the Jagiellonian idea. This was replaced by the notion of "ULB," wherein the restoration and preservation of Polish sovereignty was regarded as directly contingent on the establishment of an independent Ukraine, Lithuania and Belarus (ULB). Poland must therefore abandon all claims to the *kresy* (the eastern territories that it lost to Soviet Ukraine, Lithua-

nia and Belarus after the Molotov-Ribbentrop Pact of 1939) and establish friendly relations with the Ukrainians, Lithuanians and Belarusians.

102 The "Jagiellonian idea" refers to the geopolitical notion of a new federal state comprised of Poland, Lithuania, Ukraine and Belarus, with Warsaw as its capital. Proponents of the idea invoke the era of Jagiellonian dynastic rule (1386-1572), and, more generally, the history of the Polish-Lithuanian Commonwealth – a federative state established in 1569 as a result of the Union of Lublin between the Kingdom of Poland and the Grand Duchy of Lithuania. At its greatest extent in the first third of the seventeenth century, the Commonwealth encompassed Polish, Lithuanian, Belarusian, Ukrainian and certain Russian lands. After the restoration of the Polish state in November 1918, Józef Pilsudski developed the idea of creating a large Eastern European federation (Intermarium) under the aegis of Poland, thus emulating the Commonwealth.

103 Michnik means that they aimed to smoothen out the historical rift between the Polish and Ukrainian people; and makes an example of France and Germany, who have been fighting throughout centuries, but now are allies.

104 In the first half of the twentieth century, Poles comprised the majority of the population of Vilnius (the percentage ranging from 30 to 65%). The percentage of Poles in Lvov ranged from 50 to 63%, but, in contrast to Vilnius – the birthplace of Pilsudski and the city of Mickiewicz – Lvov was not quite as deeply rooted in the Polish national consciousness.

105 In July 2014, at the height of the Russia-backed separatist conflict in Eastern Ukraine, the Russian state-run Channel One broadcast what it said was an eyewitness account of a 3-year-old boy tortured and crucified by the Ukrainian military in a public square in Slovyansk. Investigations by independent journalists showed that the report was made up.

Alexei Navalny was one of many people who were revolted by the fabrication. "Are they completely sick to come up with something like that? ... The people who orchestrate such things are dangerous for society, and what they are doing is a crime."

106 The Budapest Memorandum is an agreement signed in 1994 by the leaders of Russia, Ukraine, the US and the UK; the document pledges respect for the "independence and sovereignty and existing borders of Ukraine" (Article 1), and affirms the signatories' "obligation to refrain from the threat or use of force" or "economic coercion" against Ukraine (Articles 2 and 3 respectively). Subsequently, the bilateral Russian-Ukrainian Treaty of Friendship, Cooperation and Partnership (1997) reaffirmed the guarantee of Ukraine's territorial integrity (Article 2).

107 After the Second World War, the Saar region, formerly part of Germany, was integrated into the French occupation zone before becoming a French protectorate in 1947. France planned to turn the Saar into an independent state under the auspices of the Western European Union while retaining control over the region's economy. On October 23, 1955, the Saarland's inhabitants rejected this plan in a referendum, with 67.7% voting against (the turnout was 96.7%). The

outcome of the referendum was interpreted as the desire on the part of a majority of Saarlanders to return to the Federal Republic of Germany. On October 27, 1956, France and the Federal Republic signed the Luxembourg Agreements, which provided for the political reintegration of the Saarland into the latter. Reunification took place on January 1, 1957.

108 Red Army captain Alexander Solzhenitsyn was arrested under Article 58 of the RSFSR Penal Code (which dealt with "counter-revolutionary crimes") on February 9th, 1945 by SMERSH counterintelligence personnel. According to the NKGB, Solzhenitsyn had "created an anti-Soviet youth group and [was] currently working on putting together an anti-Soviet organisation." On July 7 of the same year, Solzhenitsyn was sentenced to eight years in the labour camps. On completion of his sentence (9 February 1953), he was exiled indefinitely to the Kazakh SSR before being freed in 1956 (when exile for individuals convicted under Article 58 was revoked) and rehabilitated the following year.

109 The Home Army (*Armia Krajowa*), established in 1942, was the primary military force of the Polish government-in-exile. Active in Nazi-occupied Poland, it was, until 1944, primarily engaged in guerrilla, intelligence and sabotage activities. By the summer of 1944, it numbered in the region of 300,000-400,000 soldiers, and constituted the largest underground anti-fascist force in Europe. On August 1, 1944, the Home Army instigated the Warsaw uprising, which was ultimately crushed by the Germans on October 2. The Home Army was disbanded in January 1945. However,

individual units (the so-called "cursed soldiers") continued an underground struggle against the Red Army, which had occupied Polish territory.

110 "Punitive expeditioners" was a term used by Russian and Russia-backed spokesmen during the Russia backed separatist conflict in Eastern Ukraine, to describe Ukrainian forces that allegedly raided civilians' homes and looted their belongings.

111 Michnik is referring to four laws passed by Ukraine's Verkhovna Rada on April 9, 2015. These laws concern: the "Legal Status and Honouring of Fighters for Ukraine's Independence in the Twentieth Century;" the condemnation of "the communist and Nazi totalitarian regimes" and the prohibition of their propaganda symbols; the remembrance "of victory over Nazism in the Second World War;" and access to communist archives. In Russia, the following aspects of the laws received the greatest attention: the rejection of the notion of the "Great Patriotic War" (with May 9 now considered the day of victory over the Nazis, rather than Victory Day in the Great Patriotic War); the equation of the Communist and Nazi ideologies; and the laying of blame for the outbreak of the Second World War at the feet of both Germany and the Soviet Union. A group of prominent scholars from various countries penned an open letter to President Petro Poroshenko, appealing to him to reject two of the four laws (concerning the legal status of freedom fighters and the ban on communist propaganda) on the basis that "their content and spirit contradicts one of the most fundamental political rights: the right to freedom of speech." (See http://krytyka.com/en/articles/open-letter-scholars-and-

experts-ukraine-re-so-called-anti-communist-law#sthash.9i3ptjfT.dpuf). The appeal proved unsuccessful.

112 A reference to a poem by Mikhail Lermontov (1814-1841) written between 1840 and 1841, when he had been exiled to the Caucasus.

Farewell, farewell, unwashed Russia,
Land of slaves, land of lords,
And you, blue uniforms,*
And you, folks obedient to them.

Perhaps, beyond the Caucasian mountains
I'll hide myself from your pashas,
From their all-seeing eyes,
From their all-hearing ears.

* A reference to the Third Department secret police.

113 Sergei Parkhomenko's *Last Known Address* project aims "to perpetuate the memory of those among our compatriots who fell victim to political repression and state tyranny in the Soviet era." It involves the installation "of thousands of personal commemorative plaques on the facades of buildings known as the last residential addresses of these victims." The project's fundamental principle is encapsulated in the motto "One Name, One Life, One Sign."

(See http://www.poslednyadres.ru, the project's official website).

114 Navalny is referring to a paper by Anton Cheremukhin, Mikhail Golosov, Sergei Guriev, and Aleh

Tsyvinski entitled "Was Stalin necessary for Russia's economic development?" The full English-language version of the study is available here: http://www.nber.org/papers/w19425.pdf

Notes

Notes

Notes

Notes

Notes

Notes